Insects

Libby Romero

NATIONAL GEOGRAPHIC
WASHINGTON, D.C.

Contents

PYGMY MOLE CRICKET, PAGE 50

SNAKEFLY, PAGE 87

5

About Insects

INSECTS ARE INVERTEBRATES (animals without backbones) that have been around for hundreds of millions of years. They are the largest and most diverse group of animals found on Earth today.

WHAT'S THE STORY?

When people think of prehistoric animals, they often picture big creatures like dinosaurs. But insects lived back then, too. In fact, the first insects appeared around 480 million years ago. That's about 250 million years before the first dinosaurs showed up!

Insects belong to a group of animals called arthropods. Arthropods don't have internal skeletons and backbones like people do. Instead, they have an exoskeleton. An exoskeleton is a hard covering on the outside of the animal's body.

Some exoskeletons are thick and hard; others are thin and light. Some let water and gases in; others keep them out. Adaptations in the exoskeleton are one reason that insects have become the most successful animal group on Earth.

Arthropods have two other notable features that make them easy to identify. Their bodies are segmented, or divided into parts. And their arms and legs are jointed. The word *arthropod* even means "jointed leg."

WHAT IS AN INSECT?

Insects are just one type of arthropod. Others include spiders, crabs, lobsters, centipedes, and scorpions. These organisms share common traits with insects, but they're not insects. They're distant relatives. What makes an insect different?

- Insects have six legs. Other arthropods have more.
- An insect's body is divided into three main parts. Other arthropods have one or two main body sections.
- Insects usually have wings. No other arthropods have wings.

The three parts of an insect's body are the head, thorax, and abdomen. The head contains mouthparts, two antennae, and the insect's eyes.

Legs and wings attach to the thorax. Insects move their legs and wings with muscles attached to the exoskeleton on the inside of their bodies.

The abdomen is at the end of the insect's body. It contains the insect's reproductive, digestive, circulatory, and respiratory systems.

HOW INSECTS USE THEIR BODY PARTS

Just like people, insects have the senses of sight, hearing, taste, touch, and smell. But their senses work very differently than ours do.

- **Sight:** Insects can have simple eyes, compound eyes, both, or neither. Simple eyes distinguish between dark and light. Compound eyes can help insects see a wider range of colors or see in all directions.

- **Hearing:** Many insects can't hear. Those that can hear use different body parts to do so. Crickets hear with a structure called a tympanum on their front legs. Some moths can hear, too.

- **Taste:** Most insects taste with their mouthparts or their feet. Bees have taste receptors on their antennae.

- **Touch:** Insects have small hairs on their bodies. There's a nerve at the base of each hair. They can feel objects and changes in air movement around them.

- **Smell:** Insects have receptors on their antennae that detect and gather molecules of odors in the air. That's how they smell.

Common Green Darner Wings

DARK BROWN LEGS

THREE SMALL EYES BETWEEN COMPOUND EYES

GREEN FACE

COMPOUND EYES

TWO SETS OF CLEAR WINGS WITH BLACK VEINS

Cicada Eyes

THE COMMON GREEN DARNER (RIGHT) HAS TWO SETS OF WINGS.
THE CICADA (LEFT) HAS TWO LARGE COMPOUND AND THREE SMALL EYES.

A World of Insects

EUROPEAN EARWIG, PAGE 43

Insects are all around you. More than one million different species have been identified and many more have yet to be discovered. According to some estimates, there are nearly 10 quintillion insects in the world.

That's a lot of insects to keep track of. So to help people understand insects, scientists divide them into groups based on their common traits. This process is called scientific classification. All living things are categorized in this way.

Members of the Palaeoptera orders are sometimes called the "ancient winged" insects. These insects have large membranous wings. They can't fold these wings. Instead, they hold their wings straight up or out to the side. Mayflies, dragonflies, and damselflies belong to this group.

HALLOWEEN PENNANT, PAGE 20

Insects in the Orthopteroid orders have chewing mouthparts and a set of body parts called "cerci" at the end of their abdomens. These cerci may be pincers. They also have long multi-segmented antennae (European earwig, top). Most adults have four wings, and the front wings can be thick and leathery. When resting, these insects fold their front wings on top of their hind wings on their backs. Members of this group of orders, including cockroaches and grasshoppers, are usually clumsy fliers.

Specialized mouthparts are the most notable feature of insects in the Hemipteroid orders. These insects have mouths built for sucking and chewing. Some, like certain species of barklice and aphids, can cause a lot of damage. Others, such as head lice, can be truly annoying!

All insects undergo metamorphosis (see pages 14-15), or a change in form. Only members of the Holometabola orders undergo complete metamorphosis. These insects develop in four stages: egg, larva, pupa, and adult. Nearly 85 percent of all insects—including butterflies, moths, wasps, and bees—belong to this group.

SCIENTIFIC CLASSIFICATION

Scientists have classified insects and every other kind of creature in the animal kingdom using seven levels. Check out the seven classifications of a Scarab beetle:

Kingdom	Animalia (animals)
Phylum	Arthropoda (jointed legs, or more precisely, "jointed foot")
Class	Insecta (insects)
Order	Coleoptera (beetles)
Family	Scarabaeidae
Genus	*Phanaeus*
Species	*Phanaeus vindex*

Where to Find Them

Insects have adapted to live in all types of environments. They live inside and outside, in the water and on land. You can find them in hot places and cold places. Some insects even live on you!

You can find insects almost anywhere, and the more places you look, the more insects you find!

START WITH PLANTS

Caterpillars are the larvae of butterflies and moths. They can often be found on the underside of leaves. Aphids are small, soft-bodied insects that live on stems and leaves. If you happen to spot aphids, you will probably see lady beetles (aka ladybugs), too. Lady beetles eat aphids along with the pollen of certain flowers.

WESTERN TIGER SWALLOWTAIL, PAGE 126

Many insects eat pollen. Plants need these insects to transfer pollen from flower to flower. Plants even use color, shape, and scent to attract the right insects. For example, bees like shallow flowers that are bright white, yellow, and blue. Butterflies prefer flowers with bright red and purple tubes.

LOOK UP AND DOWN

If you're outside, don't forget to look up. You can see all kinds of insects flying through the air. At night, many different insects are attracted to lights. Fireflies and a few other species glow in the dark.

RAINBOW SCARAB, PAGE 97

Another great place to look is on the ground. Many insects live under rocks and logs. Some, such as mantids, are common in gardens and flower beds. And if you're not careful, you might step on a Rainbow Scarab. That wouldn't be pleasant! These beetles live in the soil underneath piles of manure.

As you're searching, don't forget about the water. Mosquitoes like moist environments and their larvae live in standing water. Water Striders live on top of ponds. The larvae of dobsonflies and fishflies live underwater for several years before they make their way to land and become pupae.

It's just as easy to find insects in and around your home. Wasps often build their nests under the eaves of houses. Occasionally, one will fly inside. If you look around, you might also find flies, crickets, moths, and any number of other insect species. Good places to look are the pantry and the basement. You'll also find insects near food, particularly fresh or decaying fruit.

WHEN TO FIND THEM

It's pretty easy to find insects during the summer months. Some can also be seen in the spring and fall. But it's much harder to spot them outside during the cold winter months. There are several reasons for that. First, some insects pass the winter months in the larva, pupa, or nymph stage. The insects are there, but they're not in the adult form that people are most likely to recognize. And they may be buried underground. Insects that are adults at this time of year have different ways of dealing with winter. Some migrate to warmer climates to avoid cold temperatures that would surely kill them. Monarch butterflies do this. Others, like the lady beetle, hibernate.

SEVEN-SPOTTED LADY BEETLE, PAGE 95

PLAYING IT SAFE

Look for this Danger! sign throughout this guide to know when an insect has a bite, a sting, or produces a chemical reaction that could harm you. If a wasp, bee, hornet, or fire ant stings you, it will hurt. If a mosquito or flea bites you, it will itch. Usually, the reaction is mild. But if you're allergic to the bite or sting, you may need medical attention. In the United States, yellowjackets cause the most allergic reactions. There are three to four times more deaths from reactions to their stings than there are from poisonous snakebites.

BITE

STING

CHEMICAL REACTION

Another issue is that some insects carry disease. In the United States, a mosquito bite can spread West Nile virus. In other parts of the world, a mosquito bite can give you malaria or some other infection.

The best way to stay safe when observing insects is to be prepared. Wear protective clothing and use insect repellent. Avoid wearing hairspray, perfume, or other scented products. Don't bother insects, and never disrupt a hive or nest. Most important, if you know you have an allergy, carry an emergency epinephrine kit with you at all times.

NORTHERN HOUSE MOSQUITO, PAGE 118

Protecting Insects

Insects are highly adaptable, and they make up about 80 percent of the animal diversity on Earth. Because of this, many people don't think about protecting and conserving insects when they clear land and use natural resources. They should.

Insects are tiny, but they play a major role in the food chain. Insects provide food for all kinds of animals, including other insects. They pollinate crops, make honey, make silk, and clean up the environment. In some parts of the world, people even eat insects for food. If insects were to disappear, the impact would be enormous.

One way to conserve insects is to protect or create habitats where they can thrive. For example, some people build butterfly gardens. To do this, find a sunny location. Make sure it's sheltered from the wind. Then choose plants that attract butterflies and plants that caterpillars can eat.

You can also help insects by reminding adults not to use chemicals near bodies of water where insects might live. Some insects are pests, and people use pesticides to keep down their populations. Unfortunately, other insects can be affected, too.

✓ CHECKLIST FOR FINDING INSECTS IN THE FIELD

Here are some things to bring along on your search for insects.

✓ BINOCULARS OR MAGNIFYING GLASS

Insects are small, so you may need help to see them. You'll want to keep your distance for stinging insects like bees and hornets. Binoculars will let you study them from a safe distance. For other types of insects, a magnifying glass will be more useful.

SOUTHERN GREEN STINK BUG, PAGE 75

✓ A GUIDE

Take this book with you on hikes, bike rides, and car trips. You also might want to get a more focused guide that includes all the species in your area.

✓ A NOTEBOOK

Pack a small notebook and pen or pencil in your backpack. You'll want to keep a record of the species you see and when and where you find them. You can even make quick sketches that will help you identify them later.

✓ PROPER CLOTHING

Wear clothes that don't make you stick out in any habitat. Earth colors like tans and greens help you blend into the surroundings. Many insects—including some that you'd prefer to avoid—are attracted to bright colors. Wear long pants, long sleeves, and sturdy shoes in the woods, meadows, and tall grass to protect against poison ivy and ticks. Wear a hat for sun protection.

HOW TO USE This Book

THIS BOOK IS ORGANIZED into two sections based on the type of metamorphosis insects go through (incomplete or complete). Species are further broken down by scientific classification within each section. Here's more on how to use this guide.

Western Carpenter Ant Page 141

Insect Entry

HERE IS THE ANIMAL'S SCIENTIFIC NAME, ITS ORDER, ITS AVERAGE LENGTH (NOT THE WORLD RECORD), THE HABITATS IT LIVES IN, AND WHERE IT LIVES IN NORTH AMERICA.

THIS IS WHERE YOU'LL FIND THE INSECT'S COMMON NAME.

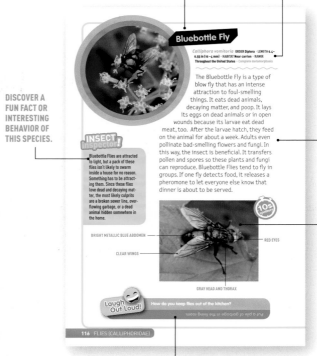

Bluebottle Fly

Calliphora vomitoria **ORDER Diptera · LENGTH 0.4–0.55 in (10 –14 mm) · HABITAT Near carrion · RANGE Throughout the United States ·** Complete metamorphosis

The Bluebottle Fly is a type of blow fly that has an intense attraction to foul-smelling things. It eats dead animals, decaying matter, and poop. It lays its eggs on dead animals or in open wounds because its larvae eat dead meat, too. After the larvae hatch, they feed on the animal for about a week. Adults even pollinate bad-smelling flowers and fungi. In this way, the insect is beneficial. It transfers pollen and spores so these plants and fungi can reproduce. Bluebottle Flies tend to fly in groups. If one fly detects food, it releases a pheromone to let everyone else know that dinner is about to be served.

THIS TEXT GIVES GENERAL INFORMATION ABOUT THE SPECIES, INCLUDING KEY BEHAVIORS AND SOME COOL, SURPRISING FACTS.

DISCOVER A FUN FACT OR INTERESTING BEHAVIOR OF THIS SPECIES.

INSECT Inspector!

Bluebottle Flies are attracted to light, but a pack of these flies isn't likely to swarm inside a house for no reason. Something has to be attracting them. Since these flies love dead and decaying matter, the most likely culprits are a broken sewer line, over-flowing garbage, or a dead animal hidden somewhere in the home.

10s

BRIGHT METALLIC BLUE ABDOMEN

CLEAR WINGS

RED EYES

GRAY HEAD AND THORAX

QUICKLY IDENTIFY AN INSECT BY LOOKING FOR THESE BASIC FEATURES. CAN YOU NAME THE CORRECT SPECIES IN 10 SECONDS?

Laugh Out Loud! How do you keep flies out of the kitchen?

Put a pile of garbage in the living room.

116 FLIES (CALLIPHORIDAE)

INSECT JOKES, PUNS, AND RIDDLES WILL MAKE YOU AND YOUR FRIENDS LAUGH. TRY THEM ON YOUR FAMILY, TOO!

SPECIAL FEATURES CALLED INSECT REPORTS give you a closer look at insects' appearance, their amazing behaviors, and their remarkable life cycles and lifestyles.

A CAPTION DESCRIBES THE MAIN PHOTO.

A TEXT BLOCK GIVES GENERAL INFORMATION ABOUT THE SPECIAL FEATURES OF APPEARANCE, BEHAVIOR, OR LIFESTYLE.

LEARN ABOUT THE DIFFERENT SPECIES THAT REPRESENT THE THEME OF THE REPORT.

Classification

Scientists describe and classify insects, just as they do all other living things. Each type of insect is a species. Closely related species are grouped together in a genus, and each genus is grouped with relatives in a family. The animals in each group share characteristics as well as common genes inherited from an ancestor. This is how each insect gets its scientific name. The scientific name is written in Latin and contains the insect's genus. A few also have a common name, or the name that non-scientists use. But most insects don't. Instead, all members of the family share the same common name. To help you identify insects, the common and scientific family names are found in a classification tab at the bottom margin of the pages. For those insects that don't have a specific common name, only the scientific name is used.

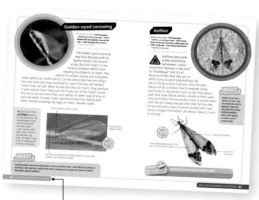

CLASSIFICATION TAB

METAMORPHOSIS

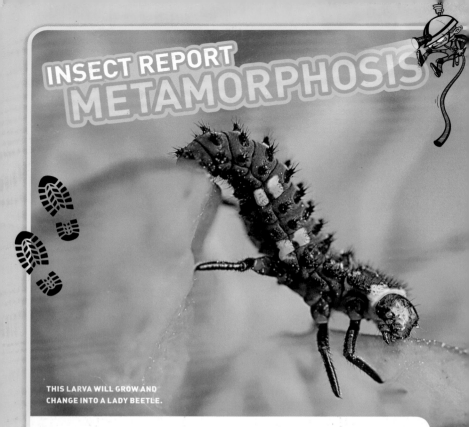

THIS LARVA WILL GROW AND
CHANGE INTO A LADY BEETLE.

All insects begin life inside an egg. After hatching from an egg, a young insect starts to grow. Its exoskeleton does not, and soon that outer covering becomes too tight. The insect molts, or sheds its old skin. Then it continues to grow and change as it develops into an adult. This process is called metamorphosis. There are two types of metamorphosis—simple (incomplete) and complete. Species like grasshoppers and dragonflies undergo simple metamorphosis, which has three stages: egg, nymph, and adult. Other insects, like butterflies and beetles, go through complete metamorphosis. There are four stages in that process: egg, larva, pupa, and adult.

INCOMPLETE METAMORPHOSIS: Grasshopper

❶ Female grasshoppers lay eggs in the soil in the fall. ❷ Protective pods help the eggs survive through winter. ❸ In the spring, eggs hatch and nymphs emerge. Nymphs eat and grow. They molt several times. ❹ Within two months, the nymphs become adults with fully developed wings.

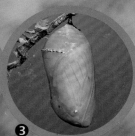

COMPLETE METAMORPHOSIS: Butterfly

❶ A caterpillar develops inside an egg. ❷ After 3 to 15 days, the caterpillar hatches from the egg. The larva feeds and grows for about two weeks. It molts five times. ❸ Then the caterpillar turns into a pupa. ❹z Two weeks later, an adult butterfly emerges.

Giant Mayfly

Hexagenia limbata **ORDER Ephemeroptera**
• LENGTH 0.34–1.07 in (8.5–27 mm) • HABITAT Lakes and
rivers with sandy or gravel bottoms • RANGE Widespread
throughout the United States and Canada, except Arizona
and Alaska • Incomplete metamorphosis

Mayflies tend to have short life spans, but the Giant Mayfly takes that to the extreme. A Giant Mayfly nymph takes about two years to develop. The nymph digs a u-shaped burrow in the bottom of a shallow lake or river. There, it molts up to 30 times. When it's ready, the nymph catches a ride to the surface on a bubble of air. It molts into an immature adult and flies to land. A day or two later, it molts again to become a mature adult. But time is short! Giant Mayfly adults have just two days to mate and lay eggs. Then they die. As adults, these insects are so focused on reproduction that they don't even have mouthparts that can eat!

LONG FRONT LEGS

LARGE COMPOUND EYES

VEINED WINGS POINT STRAIGHT UP

TWO HAIRLIKE TAILS

10s spotters

Laugh Out Loud! What do you call a mayfly that's always late?

A June bug.

Common Green Darner

GREEN THORAX

Anax junius ORDER **Odonata** · LENGTH **2.75–3.15 in (70–80 mm)** · HABITAT **Nymphs live in lakes, ponds, and slow streams; adults on land but need a nearby water supply** · RANGE **The entire United States, north into southern Canada and south into parts of Mexico** · Incomplete metamorphosis

LONG, THIN ABDOMEN WITH BLACK STRIPE

OUTSTRETCHED WINGS

The Common Green Darner is a type of dragonfly named for its long, thin abdomen that looks like a darning needle. These dragonflies are daytime eaters that fly through the air catching a variety of insects, including mosquitoes. Like all dragonflies, Common Green Darners have four wings, which are attached to the thorax. Some Common Green Darners stay in the general area where they were born. Others may migrate thousands of miles away. That's why Common Green Darners are found in just about every type of habitat.

→ LOOK FOR THIS

COMMON GREEN DARNERS are a colorful species. Males have dull green eyes, a green face, and a bright green thorax. The abdomen is green, turning to bright blue, and fading to dark green at the end. There are two types of females. Most have a green abdomen, brown top, and grayish green sides. But some look just like the males.

GREEN FACE   DARK BROWN LEGS

Giant Darner

Anax walsinghami ORDER **Odonata** · LENGTH **3.5–4.6 in (89–117 mm)** · HABITAT **Ponds, streams, and marshes** · RANGE **Southwestern United States, Mexico, Guatemala, and Honduras** · Incomplete metamorphosis

This darner is the largest of the 450 species of dragonflies in the United States. It grows up to 4.6 inches (117 mm) long, with a wing spread nearly 6 inches (152 mm) wide. Its green abdomen has metallic blue spots. A fast flier, it also hovers over water like a helicopter!

TWO SETS OF CLEAR WINGS WITH BLACK VEINS

ABDOMEN CURVES DOWNWARD.

INSECT inspector!

The nymphs of mayflies and dragonflies are called "naiads." Most dragonfly naiads can move by jet propulsion. They rapidly contract their rectal muscles to squirt water out their rear ends. This shoots them forward in the water.

Twin-spotted Spiketail

Cordulegaster maculata **ORDER Odonata**
• **LENGTH 2.5–3 in (63.5–76 mm)** • **HABITAT Clear forest streams and rivers** • **RANGE Eastern United States and southeastern Canada** • Incomplete metamorphosis

The Twin-spotted Spiketail is a large blackish brown dragonfly that has rows of bright yellow spots shaped like rounded triangles on its abdomen. Its eyes are bluish green. Like all spiketails, it has a wide head and clear to smoky black wings. Males have slightly club-shaped abdomens and can often be seen patrolling up and down the middle of streams. Females hover vertically just over the surface of the water and repeatedly dip their abdomens into the water to deposit eggs. This movement, called spiking, gives this group of dragonflies its name. Unlike darners, which perch vertically, spiketails hang from an angle on plants and twigs.

10s spotters

BLUISH GREEN EYES

BLACKISH BROWN BODY   **ROWS OF YELLOW SPOTS**

Laugh Out Loud!   Why was the knight running?

He saw a dragonfly!

Cobra Clubtail

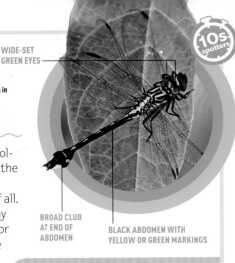

Gomphus vastus ORDER **Odonata** • LENGTH **1.9–2.25 in (48.5–57 mm)** • HABITAT **Large sandy-bottomed rivers and large, windswept lakes** • RANGE **Eastern United States and southeastern Canada** • *Incomplete metamorphosis*

WIDE-SET GREEN EYES

BROAD CLUB AT END OF ABDOMEN

BLACK ABDOMEN WITH YELLOW OR GREEN MARKINGS

All clubtail dragonflies have a swollen part that looks like a club at the tip of their abdomen. The Cobra Clubtail has the broadest club of all. Scientists don't know exactly why this part is swollen. It could be for display, or perhaps it helps these insects fly. Cobra Clubtails have black abdomens with pale yellow to green markings. Their wide-set eyes are bright green and they have a black stripe on their face. No other clubtail has this marking.

DON'T BE FOOLED The long, thin abdomen on a dragonfly looks like a stinger, and scary-sounding names like Cobra Clubtail don't help. But there's no need to worry. Dragonflies are perfectly harmless to people. If you were a fly or mosquito, however, it would be a different story. Like all members of the order Odonata, dragonflies have teeth!

Flag-tailed Spinyleg

YELLOW-GREEN THORAX; BLACK SHOULDER STRIPES

FLATTENED CLUB

COMBLIKE SPIKES (ON LEGS)

Dromogomphus spoliatus ORDER **Odonata** • LENGTH **2.2–2.6 in (56–66 mm)** • HABITAT **Slow rivers and streams, large ponds** • RANGE **Midwest and south-central United States**

The Flag-tailed Spinyleg is one of three spiny-leg species found in the United States. Not only do these dragonflies have clubs at the end of their abdomens, their back legs are also armed with 4 to 11 long, comblike spikes! These spines help them capture prey. The Flag-tailed Spinyleg has a yellow-green thorax with black shoulder stripes. Its abdomen has black rings. The club on males is flattened vertically and is colored yellow to rusty orange. The female's club looks like the male's, but it's smaller.

Halloween Pennant

Celithemis eponina **ORDER** Odonata · **LENGTH** 1.2–1.65 in
(30.5–42 mm) · **HABITAT** Lakes, ponds, borrow pits, and marshes with
emergent vegetation · **RANGE** Widespread throughout eastern United
States and Canada · Incomplete metamorphosis

Orange-tinted wings with black bands
make the Halloween Pennant easy to
spot. And these colors and patterns
also explain how this dragonfly got its
name. Adult males have a red face,
stigma, and markings on the top of the
abdomen. These areas are yellow on
females and young males. Halloween
Pennants like to sit on bare twigs,
where they perch and wait for a tasty
mosquito, fly, or gnat to fly by. As they
wait, they move back and forth in the
breeze like a flag or pennant. While
most dragonflies avoid wind and rain,
those weather conditions don't seem
to bother the Halloween Pennant.
These dragonflies will even mate on
windy days and fly together as the
female deposits the eggs.

MAKE THIS!

Dragonflies are easy to draw if
you follow these simple steps.

1. Thorax: Draw a small oval.

2. Head: Draw a squashed circle
on top of the oval.

3. Eyes: Draw two small circles
inside the head circle. They
should touch in the middle. Then
draw a smaller circle inside each
of those circles.

4. Abdomen: Draw a long,
thin oval straight down from
the thorax. It should be skinnier
toward the end. Then draw lines
across the oval to show segments
on the abdomen.

5. Wings: Draw two misshapen
ovals on each side of the thorax
oval. They should look a little bit
like pea pods. Then draw lines
inside these shapes to give the
wings veins.

6. Legs: Draw lines where the
head meets the thorax and at
the top and bottom of the thorax.
Remember to make the legs
bend!

RED FACE ON MALES

SMALL, SHORT
ANTENNAE

10 s
spotters

ORANGE-TINTED WINGS
WITH BLACK BANDS AT TIPS

Ebony Jewelwing

FEMALES HAVE A WHITE SPOT ON WINGTIPS.

MALES HAVE A METALLIC GREEN BODY.

BLACK WINGS

Calopteryx maculata ORDER **Odonata** · LENGTH **1.5–2.2 in (38–56 mm)** · HABITAT **Small, slow-moving streams** · RANGE **Eastern United States and Canada** · Incomplete metamorphosis

Although the Ebony Jewelwing may look like a dragonfly, it's not. This metallic green insect with stark black wings is a damselfly. Unlike most damselflies, the Ebony Jewelwing is bigger than many dragonflies. And it flutters like a butterfly when it flies. Females have slightly lighter-colored bodies than males. They also have a white spot at the end of their wings. When courting, the female uses her wings to communicate with the male. If she quickly opens and closes her wings, she accepts him. If she leaves her wings open, it's time for him to move on.

→ **LOOK FOR THIS**

ONE WAY TO TELL if an insect is a dragonfly or damselfly is to look at the eyes. A damselfly's eyes are set farther apart. You can also look at the wings. An adult dragonfly's hind wings are broader than the front wings. They rest their wings to the side. An adult damselfly's front and hind wings have similar shapes. When resting, they bring their wings together above their back.

American Rubyspot

SPOT AT BASE OF WINGS IS RED IN MALES (AMBER IN FEMALES).

Hetaerina americana ORDER **Odonata** · LENGTH **1.5–1.8 in (38–45.5 mm)** · HABITAT **Wide-open streams and river** · RANGE **Throughout North America, south through Mexico, Guatemala, and Honduras** · Incomplete metamorphosis

MALES HAVE A METALLIC RED THORAX AND HEAD (FEMALES' ARE METALLIC GREEN).

Another showy damselfly is the American Rubyspot. Males of this species have a metallic red head and thorax. On females, these parts are a metallic green. Both males and females have a large spot at the base of their wings. On the female, that spot is amber. On the male, it's red. For males, these spots are thought to help with communication. Males constantly defend their territories along rivers and streams. Those with larger red spots have been found to be more successful in battle than their smaller-spotted foes.

MALE EYES, FACE
ARE BLUE.

Great Spreadwing

Archilestes grandis ORDER **Odonata** • LENGTH **2–2.4 in
(51–61 mm)** • HABITAT **Small slow-moving streams, wetlands, and ponds**
• RANGE **Throughout the United States, south into Mexico and Central
America** • **Incomplete metamorphosis**

MALE THORAX HAS
YELLOW STRIPES.

MALE ABDOMEN
HAS BLUE-GRAY TIP.

INSECT Inspector!

Up until the 1920s, the Great
Spreadwing was only found in the
southwestern United States. Now, it's
common throughout the country. It is
the largest damselfly in the nation.

Like all spreadwings, the Great Speadwing
holds its wings slightly open when at rest.
This is unusual for a damselfly, as most
hold their wings together when they rest.
The Great Spreadwing has a long, slender
body. The male's thorax is a dull greenish
bronze with yellow stripes on the sides.
Its dark abdomen has a blue-gray tip and
its eyes and face are blue. The female's
body has more brown than the male's. The
flight season for these damselflies is
early August to mid-October.

DARK SPOTS ON LOWER THORAX

Spotted Spreadwing

Lestes congener ORDER **Odonata** • LENGTH **1.2–1.7 in (30.5–43 mm)**
• HABITAT **Ponds, lakes, marshes, and pools of stagnant or saline water**
• RANGE **Throughout the United States and Canada** • **Incomplete
metamorphosis**

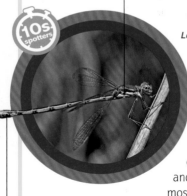

BLUE GRAY TIP ON
END OF ABDOMEN

The Spotted Spreadwing is found
throughout the United States, fre-
quenting shallow marshes and ponds. Its
naiads, or nymphs, are active predators,
eating the larvae of mosquitoes, mayflies,
and other aquatic insects. An adult hunts
mosquitoes, flies, and moths. It has one of the
latest flight seasons of all damselflies. That is
because its eggs go dormant through the win-
ter months, and then develop again when temperatures warm up in
the spring. This causes the eggs to hatch later in the summer than
other spreadwings,' which pushes back their flight season.

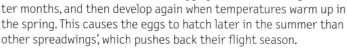

Powdered Dancer

Argia moesta ORDER **Odonata** • LENGTH **1.5–1.7 in (38–43 mm)** • HABITAT **Rocky streams, rivers, and lakes** • RANGE **Most of the United States, southeastern Canada, northern Mexico** • Incomplete metamorphosis

SOME FEMALES HAVE A BLUE HEAD, THORAX.

MALE THORAX IS WHITE; IMMATURE MALES ARE TAN WITH TWO BROAD, DARK STRIPES.

In most of nature, the male members of a species are more brightly colored than the females. Damselflies are no exception. But the Powdered Dancer is one of the few damselflies to break that trend. Male Powdered Dancers develop a waxy, light-colored substance that makes their dark bodies look white, particularly. Females don't. And the females come in two distinct color variations. Some have a light blue head and thorax. Others are brown with a greenish tint.

→ LOOK FOR THIS
WITH SOME 1,000 SPECIES, Coenagrionidae is the largest family of damselflies. Its members have narrow wings that lack color. They are usually 1-2 inches (25.5–51 mm) long and their bodies may be green, blue, yellow, orange, or purple. They are usually found near ponds and other still water. Some, like the dancers, prefer stream habitats.

TOP HALF OF THORAX AND ABDOMEN IS BLACK; IN MALES LOWER HALF IS IRIDESCENT GREEN.

Black-fronted Forktail

Ischnura denticollis ORDER **Odonata** • LENGTH **0.9–1 in (23–25.5 mm)** • HABITAT **Spring-fed pools and streams in arid areas** • RANGE **Eastern Oregon east to Kansas and south to Texas, Baja California, and Guatemala** • Incomplete metamorphosis

Measuring an inch long—the size of a small paper clip—the Black-fronted Forktail is a tiny damselfly. Males are black on top with iridescent green on the sides. The tip of the tail and lower sides of the thorax are blue. Most females are light orange-brown, but some look like the males. This species is common in the western United States.

ALL HAVE SMALL BLUE SPOTS ON TIP OF ABDOMEN/TAIL.

MALES HAVE SMALL BLUE SPOTS NEAR EYES.

Laugh Out Loud!

Which part did the Powdered Dancer audition for in the school play?

The damsel(fly) in distress.

INSECT REPORT
JUST WING IT!

A NETWORK OF VEINS RUNS THROUGH AN INSECT'S WINGS. THESE VEINS HELP TO STRENGTHEN THE WINGS, AND THE PATTERN IS USEFUL FOR IDENTIFICATION.

Insects are the only invertebrates that can fly. How well an insect flies depends on the type of wings it has. Wings can be thick or thin. They can be leathery, scaly, or smooth. Some wings are just used for flying. Others are adapted to protect the insect's body, collect heat, and even attract mates. Although most adult insects have two pairs of wings, some have one pair and others have none.

Butterfly

This is a close-up of a butterfly's wing. It is covered with flattened scales. The fine texture on each scale creates the color we see.

House fly

A house fly has small, club-like hind wings (called "halters") that stabilize the insect during flight.

Thrip

Thrips have long fringes of hair on their wings. When they fly, they look like they're swimming through the air!

Beetle

Beetles have hard, thick front wings. They protect the membranous hind wings, which beetles use to fly.

Giant Salmonfly

Pteronarcys californica ORDER **Plecoptera**
• **LENGTH 1.2–2 in (30.5–51 mm)** • **HABITAT Fast-moving mountain streams or large-to-medium-size rivers below 7,000 ft (2,134 m)** • **RANGE Western and northwestern United States and Canada, including Alaska** • Incomplete metamorphosis

With a body nearly 2 inches (51 mm) long and a wingspan exceeding 3 inches (76 mm), the Giant Salmonfly is hard to miss. It's the largest stonefly in the United States. Nymphs wait for the water temperature to be just right, usually between late May and early July. Then they crawl out from under rocks on the bottom of rivers and streams and make their way to land. If the air temperature is too cold, they will die. Once on land, they finish developing into winged adults and become completely focused on reproduction. Males drum on rocks or wood to attract females' attention. They have to move quickly. Some adults live a few weeks, but many die after one or two days.

INSECT Inspector!

Unlike other insect nymphs that live in the water, stonefly nymphs have two stout tails and dual wing pads on the thorax. The Giant Salmonfly nymph is easy to recognize because of its large chocolate brown body. In addition, it has branched, fluffy gills sticking out between its legs that look like hairy armpits!

ORANGE BAND BEHIND HEAD

DARK BROWN BODY

BROAD WINGS WITH DARK VEINS

10s spotters

→ LOOK FOR THIS
THE GIANT SALMONFLY is pretty easy to spot along rivers in western North America. As an adult, it has brightly colored bands behind its head and on the underside of its abdomen. And its broad wings are covered with so many crossveins that they look like a net. Because of its size, this large stonefly is a slow, erratic flier. That makes it easy pickings for trout and birds living in and along the river.

Common Snowfly

Allocapnia granulata **ORDER Plecoptera** • **LENGTH 0.2–0.3 in (5–7.5 mm)** • **HABITAT Rocky freshwater streams and rivers** • **RANGE Northeastern United States and southern Canada to central Oklahoma** • Incomplete metamorphosis

FLAT BODY WITH LEGS WIDELY SEPARATED

LONG ANTENNAE

The Common Snowfly is an anomaly among insects. Insects are cold-blooded animals. Typically they hibernate, seek shelter, or migrate to warmer climates so they can survive the winter months. This little stonefly takes a different route. When water temperatures begin to warm up in the summer, nymphs bury themselves in the streambed. When temperatures begin to fall and the water cools down, they emerge and start to eat and grow again. Once winter hits, the nymphs become adults. They make their way through holes or cracks in the ice. A chemical similar to antifreeze in their blood keeps them warm as they walk around the snow in search of a mate.

FLAT BODY WITH LEGS WIDELY SEPARATED

Arapahoe Snowfly

Capnia arapahoe **ORDER Plecoptera** • **LENGTH 0.2 in (5 mm)** • **HABITAT Cold, clean, well-oxygenated streams and rivers** • **RANGE Larimer County, Colorado** • Incomplete metamorphosis

LONG ANTENNAE

Unlike the Common Snowfly, which has an extensive range, the Arapahoe Stonefly is found only in two small streams in Colorado. Snowfly larvae require high levels of dissolved oxygen to breathe. Oxygen levels decrease when water is polluted. Unfortunately for this tiny dark snowfly, a small lake has been constructed at the headwaters of one stream where it is found and the other stream is used extensively for recreation. Although recognized as an animal in danger of going extinct, the Arapahoe Snowfly has yet to be added to the endangered species list.

Giant Walkingstick

Megaphasma denticrus ORDER **Phasmida**
- LENGTH **3–6 in (76–152 mm)** • HABITAT **Woods, forests, and grasslands** • RANGE **Southern United States, particularly Texas; as far north as Indiana and Iowa**
- Incomplete metamorphosis

The Giant Walkingstick is the largest insect in North America. With a long, thin body colored greenish to reddish brown, it's an excellent example of mimicry in nature. This insect's body is camouflaged to look like a twig. Pulling that off is easy, considering the Giant Walkingstick moves very slowly and often sits motionless. That's necessary because adults have no wings, so they can't just fly away from danger. Although Giant Walkingsticks eat grasses and woody plants, overall they're not very destructive. That's because there aren't a ton of them around. It's easy to keep the population in check when there may be only one male for every 1,000 females in the forest!

Once in a while the camouflage doesn't work and a Giant Walkingstick loses an arm or a leg to a predator. But that's nothing to worry about. Walkingsticks can regrow missing limbs when they molt!

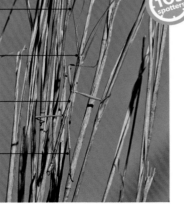

10s spotters

TWO LARGE ANTENNAE

BLENDS INTO SURROUNDINGS

GREENISH TO REDDISH BROWN BODY

SIX PALE LEGS (COUNT THEM!)

Common Walkingstick

Diapheromera femorata ORDER **Phasmida**
◦ **LENGTH 2.5–3.5 in (63.5–89 mm)** ◦ **HABITAT Deciduous woods and forests, agricultural fields, urban gardens, yards** ◦ **RANGE Eastern United States and Canada, as far west as New Mexico** ◦ **Incomplete metamorphosis**

The Common Walkingstick, as its name suggests, is the most common walkingstick in the United States. It's also the only stick insect found in Canada. Because of its long cylindrical shape, this insect has been given different names in different parts of the country: Stickbug, prairie alligator, witch's horse, northern walkingstick, and devil's darning needle are just a few. These walkingsticks have small, square heads. Their antennae are about two-thirds as long as their bodies. Even their eggs are camouflaged. They look like tiny brown seeds. Newly hatched nymphs are mini green versions of the adults. They turn brown as they grow.

→ **LOOK FOR THIS**
COMMON WALKINGSTICKS eat a whole lot and prefer oak and hazelnut trees. They eat every part of the leaf except the vein, making leaves look like skeletons. When populations are high, this can kill entire tree branches and has caused considerable damage to oak forests in the Ozark Mountains of Arkansas and Missouri.

— BROWN, GREEN, OR MULTICOLORED BODY

— SMALL, SQUARE HEAD

10s spotters

What do you call a walkingstick that takes up jogging?

An overachiever.

Laugh Out Loud!

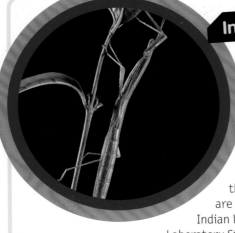

Indian Walkingstick

Carausius morosus ORDER **Phasmida** ◦ **LENGTH 2.7–4 in (68.5–101.5 mm)** ◦ **HABITAT Tropical environments** ◦ **RANGE Native in southern India; invasive in southern and central California coasts, particularly near San Diego** ◦ **Incomplete metamorphosis**

In 1991, the first Indian Walkingstick was sighted in San Diego County, California. Since then, the population of these insects has exploded. They are now considered to be pests. Indian Walkingsticks, also called the Laboratory Stick Insect, are easy to take care of. They are often kept in laboratories for research, and their one-year life span makes them popular in schools as class pets. However, like many walkingsticks, females don't need a male to reproduce. During their lifetime, they lay several hundred fertilized eggs all on their own. The eggs spread easily and hatch in 10 to 12 weeks at room temperature. The worst environmental damage occurs in the springtime, when newly hatched nymphs set out to feed on a wide variety of plants.

INSECT inspector!

Astronauts have nothing on the Indian Walkingstick. This insect has been used in outer space experiments conducted on Apollo 17 (December 1972), the Apollo-Soyuz mission (July 1975), the D1 Spacelab mission (November 1985), and the space shuttle *Atlantis* (January 1992).

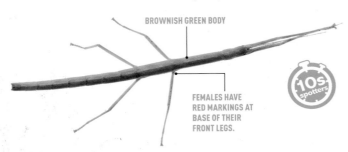

BROWNISH GREEN BODY

FEMALES HAVE RED MARKINGS AT BASE OF THEIR FRONT LEGS.

10s spotters

→ **LOOK FOR THIS**
CHINESE WALKINGSTICKS can retract their legs and hold them against their bodies. When they do this, their front legs point forward, making them look longer than they really are.

Southern Two-striped Walkingstick

Anisomorpha buprestoides ORDER **Phasmida**
- LENGTH **2–3.1 in (51–79 mm)** - HABITAT **Arid and sandy areas to highly vegetative, humid environments** - RANGE **Southeastern United States, primarily Florida** - **Incomplete metamorphosis**

OVAL-SHAPED HEAD

10s spotters

Few walkingsticks can defend themselves like the Southern Two-striped Walkingstick does. When predators approach, this phasmid shoots a stinky, milky white, acidic chemical out of two pores on its thorax, just behind the head. It has accurate aim nearly 16 inches (40.5 cm) away! Depending on where it lives, this insect's body may be brown and white or orange and white. Either way, it has two black stripes down its back. Like all walkingsticks, the Southern Two-Striped is a herbivore. It likes to munch on willows, oaks, and other leafy plants.

PORES BEHIND HEAD ON THORAX SHOOT OUT STINKY CHEMICAL.

TWO BLACK STRIPES DOWN BACK

→ LOOK FOR THIS

EARLY SCIENTISTS thought male and female Southern Two-Striped Walkingsticks were two different species. Females are much longer and wider than males. But if you find one, you'll likely find the other. These females are constantly carrying the males around on their backs.

PORES BEHIND ITS HEAD SHOOT OUT STINKY CHEMICAL.

Northern Two-striped Walkingstick

10s spotters

Anisomorpha ferruginea ORDER **Phasmida** - LENGTH **1–2.25 in (25.5–57 mm)** - HABITAT **Trees, bushes, and open areas** - RANGE **Southeastern United States north of Florida up to Pennsylvania** - **Incomplete metamorphosis**

With males just 1 to 1.5 inches (25.5 – 38 mm) long and females growing to 2.25 inches (57 mm), the Northern Two-striped Walkingstick is much smaller than its southern cousin. It has paler colors, too. They are tan, brown, or brownish yellow with stripes on their sides and down their backs. If threatened, they squirt out a powerful liquid!

STRIPE DOWN MIDDLE OF BACK AND ON SIDES

BROWNISH COLORED BODY

DANGER!

If you happen to get squirted, flush your face with lots of water right away. If the pain continues or your eyes won't focus, see a doctor right away.

Christina's Timema

Timema cristinae ORDER **Phasmida** ▪ LENGTH **0.8 in (20.5 mm)** ▪ HABITAT **Chaparral, or dense thickets** ▪ RANGE **Southern California** ▪ **Incomplete metamorphosis**

Christina's Timema is a small walkingstick that hides on a host plant at night and comes out during the night to feed. Females drop their eggs on the ground, like most walkingsticks do. But when these eggs hatch, nymphs climb to a nearby host plant and stay— sometimes for their entire lives. When Christina's Timema was first discovered, scientists noticed that it came in two color variations. Some were plain green. Others had a white stripe down their backs. The nymphs adapted to the color of the plant they were on. Scientists now consider Christina's Timema to be a perfect example of natural selection and believe the insect is evolving into two unique species.

BODY: PLAIN GREEN OR GREEN WITH A LONG WHITE STRIPE ON THE BACK

BROWN CERCI (PINCERS) AT END OF ABDOMEN

TWO BROWN ANTENNAE

BROWN LEGS

10S spotters

MAKE THIS!

Observe insects and take notes on where you found them to create an insect habitat map.

1. Go outside and walk around. Make a list of all the different insects you see. Describe where you saw each one.

2. Get a piece of paper and draw a map of the area you just toured. Draw a picture of each insect you saw or write its name. Be sure to put this information in the right location!

3. Share your map with a friend. Brainstorm ideas about why some insects live on the ground but others live on plants or up in trees.

Laugh Out Loud!

Why did the walkingstick leave the cherry tree?

It was a lousy host.

Carolina Mantis

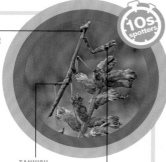

LARGE HEAD
WITH RECTANGULAR
FACEPLATE

Stagmomantis carolina ORDER **Mantodea** ▪ LENGTH **1.6–2.75 in
(40.5–70 mm)** ▪ HABITAT **Woodlands and meadows, especially around
flowering plants** ▪ RANGE **New Jersey west to Missouri and south to Mexico
and Central America** ▪ Incomplete metamorphosis

If you spot a Carolina Mantis, it's likely sitting with its front legs bent in a prayer position. Don't let that serene position fool you. This mantid is ready to strike! It sits and waits for prey to approach. Then it quickly snatches the victim with its forelegs. Ants and spiders are favorite foods, but that prey may be another mantid. Mantids are cannibals! Nymphs and adults eat each other. And females may devour the males after mating. Why is she so hungry? Females produce one or more egg pods. Each one weighs about one-third of her body weight.

TANNISH
BROWN
BODY

LARGE SERRATED,
SPINY FORELEGS
THAT FOLD BACK

→ LOOK FOR THIS
MANTIDS have widely spaced eyes that give them great depth perception. They can also turn their heads far enough to scan the full 360 degrees of their surroundings. This allows them to search for incoming predators and prey without moving the rest of their body.

Brunner's Mantis

Brunneria borealis ORDER **Mantodea** ▪ LENGTH **2.5–3.5 in
(63.5–89 mm)** ▪ HABITAT **Meadows with tall grass** ▪ RANGE **North Carolina
west to Texas, south into Mexico** ▪ Incomplete metamorphosis

ELONGATED GREEN BODY

Brunner's Mantis has a long green and pink body that looks like a walkingstick. But its raptorlike forelimbs prove that this insect is a true mantid. If you spot one of these flightless insects, you'll be looking at a female. There are no males of this species. Females can reproduce alone. They lay eggs in an egg case. The hatched nymphs look like adults.

The nymphs of most mantid species leave the egg case through separate holes that they each make for themselves. Nymphs of the Brunner's Mantis all leave through the hornlike point at the end of the egg case. They don't leave at once. It can take up to four months for all the nymphs to emerge.

10s spotters

LONG, THIN
ANTENNAE

European Mantis

Mantis religiosa ORDER **Mantodea** • LENGTH **2.5–3.2 in (63.5–81.5 mm)** • HABITAT **A variety of habitats, particularly sunny areas with lots of shrubs and plants** • RANGE **Northeastern United States to Pacific Northwest and across Canada** • Incomplete metamorphosis

LARGE SERRATED,
SPINY FORELEGS THAT
FOLD BACK

FULLY GREEN
FOREWINGS

INSECT inspector!

The Greek word *mantis* means "prophet." The term "praying mantis" was first used to describe the European mantis *(Mantis religiosa),* because these insects hold their forelegs in the praying position. That's why the common name is spelled with an "a" (pray) and not an "e" (prey).

This native of southern Europe was accidentally introduced to the United States in 1899 on a shipment of nursery plants. At first, the European Mantis was welcomed. It eats gypsy moth caterpillars, which can be highly destructive. It didn't take long for people to realize that their numbers were too small to have any impact on the moth populations. These mantids are common throughout the United States. They are typically green or brown and can be identified by the bull's-eye patterns in the "armpit" area under their front legs.

TRIANGULAR
HEAD

10s spotters

Chinese Mantis

Tenodera sinensis ORDER **Odonata** • LENGTH **3–5 in (76–127 mm)** • HABITAT **Vegetation around homes, grasslands, meadows, and agricultural areas** • RANGE **Southern and southwestern United States** • Incomplete metamorphosis

LARGE SERRATED,
SPINY FORELEGS
THAT FOLD BACK

GREEN COLOR ONLY ALONG
EDGE OF FRONT WING

WINGS EXTEND FULL
LENGTH OF BODY

The Chinese Mantis is another introduced species, brought in by gardeners in 1896 to eat insect pests. Females lay foamy masses of eggs on branches. When these masses dry, they become hard brown nuggets that may be as big as a Ping-Pong ball! Farmers and gardeners still purchase their egg cases to control pests, but these big mantids are also a concern. They will eat anything they can grab, including small reptiles and hummingbirds.

Oriental Cockroach

Blatta orientalis ORDER **Blattodea** • LENGTH **0.8–1 in (20.5–25.5 mm)** • HABITAT **Outdoors in sewers and under debris; indoors in basements and crawl spaces** • RANGE **Throughout the United States**
• Incomplete metamorphosis

The Oriental Cockroach is thought to have originated in Africa or southern Russia. These flightless cockroaches are about an inch (25.5 mm) long and have a smooth, dark, greasy-looking body. They produce an unpleasant odor. The female lays about 16 eggs at a time, lined up in pairs inside an egg case. She carries the egg case around for about 30 hours and then drops it in a warm, dry place close to food. The eggs hatch in about two months. The female lives up to 26 weeks, producing about eight egg cases and 200 young.

NARROW, LEATHERY, THICK OUTER WINGS

SMOOTH, DARK BODY

INSECT inspector!

Oriental cockroaches feed on filth, garbage, and decaying matter. They easily pick up germs, which they transfer to food and utensils in homes. Reports show that cockroaches like these have spread at least 33 kinds of bacteria, six kinds of parasitic worms, and seven other kinds of human pathogens. Cockroaches are also the fourth most common allergen.

American Cockroach

MALE WINGS EXTEND BEYOND THE TIP OF THE ABDOMEN.

REDDISH BROWN BODY

PALE BROWN TO YELLOWISH EDGE OF THE PRONOTAL SHIELD (A PLATE AT THE TOP OF THE THORAX)

Periplaneta americana ORDER **Blattodea** • LENGTH **1.3–2.1 in (33–53.5 mm)** • HABITAT **Inside large commercial buildings such as restaurants, grocery stores, and hospitals; basements and steam tunnels** • RANGE **Throughout the United States**
• Incomplete metamorphosis

Despite its name, the American Cockroach doesn't come from North America. It was introduced to this country on ships from Africa around 1625. This pest likes warm, moist environments and frequents commercial buildings, steam tunnels, and sometimes homes. Some 5,000 cockroaches were found inside a sewer manhole! The American Cockroach is a scavenger. It prefers sweets, but it will eat paper, boots, hair, and book bindings, too.

German Cockroach

Blattella germanica • ORDER **Blattodea** • **LENGTH 0.5–0.6 in (12.5–15 mm)** • **HABITAT Warm, humid places indoors like kitchens** • **RANGE Throughout the United States** • Incomplete metamorphosis

If you spot a cockroach in your kitchen, there's a good chance it's a German Cockroach. These pests have a craving for warm places, water, and food—which makes the kitchen the ideal environment for them to thrive. In addition, this species produces the largest number of eggs per egg case and has the shortest amount of time from hatching to maturity. Plus, these cockroach moms are more protective of their egg cases than other species. They carry the cases the entire time embryos are developing inside the eggs. Because of this, more nymphs survive and grow into adults. Once an infestation gets started, it spreads very quickly. Four generations of German Cockroaches can grow within just one year.

→ LOOK FOR THIS
COCKROACHES like to hide in cracks and crevices during the day. They're more active at night. That's when they prowl around for food, water, and mates. German Cockroaches are smaller than other cockroach species, so they can conceal themselves in tighter spaces, including underneath the labels on canned foods!

LIGHT BROWN BODY AND WINGS

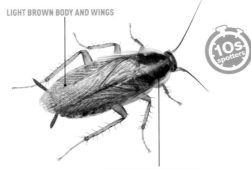

TWO BLACK STRIPES DOWN THORACIC SHIELD

10s spotters

Laugh Out Loud!

How many cockroaches does it take to screw in a lightbulb?

Nobody knows. Once the light turns on, they all run away!

Pennsylvania Wood Cockroach

Parcoblatta pennsylvanica **ORDER Blattodea** • **LENGTH 0.75–1 in (19–25.5 mm)** • **HABITAT Outdoors in woodpiles, stumps, hollow trees** • **RANGE Eastern, southern, and Midwestern United States up to Canada** • **Incomplete metamorphosis**

Not all cockroaches are indoor pests. The Pennsylvania Wood Cockroach, a native to the United States, mostly lives outdoors beneath loose bark. You can find them under woodpiles, in stumps, and in hollow trees. Although they prefer to stay outdoors, you might accidently bring one inside along with a pile of firewood. Or one might be attracted to the lights and fly inside at night. If one does make it past the front door, there's no need to worry about an infestation. These cockroaches don't reproduce indoors. They need a consistently moist environment for that to occur. And they won't eat your wooden furniture. Wood cockroaches like to feast on decaying wood and leaves.

True **or** False

Q: Cockroaches are carnivores.
A: False. Cockroaches are scavengers. They'll eat just about anything, including food, glue, leather, and even soap!

Q: Pet food can attract cockroaches.
A: True

10s. Spotters

DARK BROWN WITH LIGHT-COLORED BANDS ON THE EDGE OF THE BODY NEAR THE HEAD

FEMALE: VERY SHORT WINGS

(MALE: LONG, WELL-DEVELOPED WINGS)

→ LOOK FOR THIS
YOU CAN TELL the difference between male and female Pennsylvania Wood Cockroaches by looking at their wings. A male's wings are longer than its body. A female's wings only cover from one-third to two-thirds of her abdomen. Because of this, females can't fly. But males can fly very quickly. They just can't stay in the air for very long.

Reticulitermes flavipes **ORDER Blattodea • LENGTH 0.4 in, including wings (10 mm) • HABITAT Underground colonies • RANGE Eastern three-quarters of North America, from Maine to Florida and Montana to the Gulf Coast in Texas • Incomplete metamorphosis**

The Eastern Subterranean Termite is the most widely distributed termite in North America and, consequently, the most likely to cause damage to homes and other wooden structures. These social insects live in underground colonies with 60,000 to more than a million members. Eastern Subterranean Termites attack homes where wooden parts of the building come into direct contact with the soil. As with other termite species, there are three types of termites in the colony: workers, soldiers, and the kings and queens who reproduce.

WORKER: CREAMY WHITE AND BROWN BODY

Coptotermes formosanus **ORDER Blattodea • LENGTH 0.5–0.6 in (12.5–15 mm) • HABITAT Underground colonies • RANGE Southeastern United States to Texas, California, Hawaii • Incomplete metamorphosis**

Formosan Subterranean Termites are native to southern China. Over hundreds of years, they were transported around the world. By the 1960s, they made their way to the southern United States. These underground termites are particularly destructive because they don't just invade structures built on top of colonies. They build tunnels in the soil. These tunnels help them search for food up to 300 feet (91.5 m) from their home. In a house or other building, they build nests in walls and attics when they find the right combination of temperature and moisture.

YELLOWISH BROWN BODY

SOLDIERS HAVE TEAR-SHAPED ORANGE-BROWN HEADS, CURVED MANDIBLES.

→ LOOK FOR THIS
FORMOSAN TERMITE SOLDIERS have an opening in their heads. When attacked, they release a sticky substance through this hole. It slows down the invaders.

Southeastern Drywood Termite

Incisitermes snyderi ORDER **Blattodea**
- LENGTH **0.3–0.4 in, including wings (7.5–10 mm)**
- HABITAT **Inside large pieces of dry wood**
- RANGE **Southeastern United States** • Incomplete metamorphosis

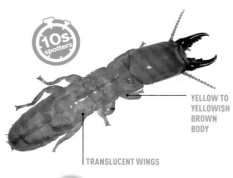

The Southeastern Drywood Termite's poop is often the first sign that the insect may be present. These termites live deep inside wood, so they're hard to see. But they squeeze every bit of water out of the wood. Then they poop very distinct six-sided fecal pellets called "frass." Termites in the colony push the frass out of the wood through tiny holes they make in the surface of the wood. The frass piles up into a mound that can look like sawdust or coffee grounds. Drywood colonies are smaller than those of other species, usually with fewer than 1,000 members. And unlike other species, there are no workers in these termite colonies. All "workers" are simply immature termites.

→ **LISTEN FOR THIS**
SUBTERRANEAN TERMITES eat wood along with the grain. Drywood termites will also eat against the grain. Sometimes, they tunnel just under the surface of the wood, causing it to look blistered. If you tap the wood with the handle of a screwdriver and it sounds hollow, you've found an infestation. If you hear a papery, rustling sound, the tunnels are just below the surface.

10s spotters

YELLOW TO YELLOWISH BROWN BODY

TRANSLUCENT WINGS

Laugh Out Loud! What did the termites name their son?

ʎpooM (Woody)

INSECT REPORT
NON-INSECT ARTHROPODS

Millipedes

Millipedes have two main body parts: a head and an abdomen. They also have lots and lots of legs! Millipedes are arthropods, but they're not insects.

THIS COMMON GREEN DARNER IS AN INSECT. IT HAS THREE BODY PARTS AND SIX LEGS.

An arthropod is an invertebrate animal with a segmented body, jointed legs, and an exoskeleton. Insects are arthropods. Their bodies are divided into three main parts—the head, thorax, and abdomen—and they have six legs. Insects also have wings. While there are millions of insects on Earth, not every little critter you see scurrying across the floor is an insect. You just have to take a look at the critter's body to understand why.

Spiders

Spiders have two main body parts: a cephalothorax, which is a combination of the head and thorax, and an abdomen. They also have eight legs. Spiders are arthropods, but they're not insects.

Ticks

Ticks have two body parts: a cephalothorax and an abdomen. Adult ticks have eight legs. Although ticks are arthropods, they're not insects.

Ring-legged Earwig

Euborellia annulipes ORDER **Dermaptera**
• LENGTH **0.5–0.75 in (12.5–19 mm)** • HABITAT **Under rocks, bark, and plant debris** • RANGE **Throughout the United States, but more common in the South and Southwest** • Incomplete metamorphosis

Ring-legged Earwigs are common insects in many areas. Like all earwigs, they are nocturnal. This species has a brownish black body with yellow stripes. Its antennae are black with white rings. Their wings are hidden, but the two pincers at the ends of the abdomen are sure to get your attention. Earwigs normally live outside, but you may see one scampering along a baseboard in your home. If you do, don't pick it up. They can pinch. And if they are crushed or feel threatened, they release a foul-smelling liquid from their scent glands. Most earwigs are scavengers. The Ring-legged Earwig is also a skilled predator, feasting on slugs, aphids, and termites.

True **or** False

Q: There are 22 species of earwigs found in the United States.
A: True

Q: The Ring-legged Earwig is native to the United States.
A: False. The Ring-legged Earwig first appeared in the United States in 1884. It is thought to have come from Europe.

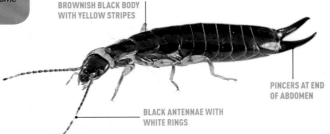

BROWNISH BLACK BODY WITH YELLOW STRIPES

PINCERS AT END OF ABDOMEN

BLACK ANTENNAE WITH WHITE RINGS

10s spotters

INSECT inspector!

Legend has it that earwigs got their name because they crawl into people's ears at night. They feast on their brains, causing madness or death. This is not true, say the experts! Other than the occasional pinch, earwigs are completely harmless to people.

European Earwig

Forficula auricularia **ORDER Dermaptera**
• **LENGTH 0.6 in (15 mm)** • **HABITAT Dark, confined,
damp areas such as under potted plants and in cracks
between pavers** • **RANGE Throughout the United
States** • Incomplete metamorphosis

The European Earwig was
first introduced to the United
States in the 1900s. Now it's
common throughout much of
the country. This flat, reddish
brown insect has very short wings. It
rarely, if ever, flies and prefers to hitchhike in bundles of newspapers, luggage, cut
flowers, and other objects. You can find them
hanging out in high-moisture areas like
around sinks, in bathtubs, or in the laundry
area. At times, large numbers of these insects
may seek shelter in and around homes. When
they do, they don't damage property but they
can be a huge nuisance because they invade
everything. You'll find them in your clothes,
furniture, clothing, and bed. You may even find
them in loaves of bread!

INSECT inspector!

Female European Earwigs
take parenthood to the
extreme—for an insect. The
mother grooms and turns her
eggs, regularly shifting their
position. Once the eggs
hatch, she guards the
nymphs and feeds them until
they have molted three
times. She doesn't eat that
whole time.

10s spotters

WINGS FOLDED
UNDER WING PADS
ON THE THORAX

YELLOW-BROWN LEGS

DARK REDDISH BROWN
BODY AND HEAD

→ LOOK FOR THIS
EUROPEAN EARWIGS HAVE a strong pair of pincers, or cerci, on the end of their abdomen. They use their cerci to
grab and hold onto prey. You can use them to separate the males from the females. On a male, the cerci are thick,
curved, and separated quite far apart at the base. On a female, the cerci are thin, straight, and close together.

Shore Earwig

Labidura riparia **ORDER Dermaptera**
• **LENGTH 0.6–1.2 in (15–30.5 mm)** • **HABITAT Farmland,
woods, and the banks of rivers, ponds, and lakes**
• **RANGE Southern United States** • Incomplete
metamorphosis

The Shore Earwig has modified cerci that work like forceps. If those don't keep predators at bay, the foul-smelling odor it spits out surely will. It smells like rotting flesh! In one study, researchers saw a lizard attack a Shore Earwig. The earwig released the smell, and the lizard fled. It didn't bother any Shore Earwigs for several weeks. Talk about learning a lesson! Shore Earwigs have tan to dark brown bodies. They like dark, moist environments where they can hide during the day. When it's time to build a nest, they'll often take over abandoned mole cricket burrows. If the nest is destroyed, they may fly to find a new home.

INSECT inspector!

Shore Earwigs are ravenous predators that eat nearly every type of insect. These earwigs often seize larger insects with their forceps and quickly attack with their mouths. One specimen can devour 20 to 25 larvae in a night.

10s spotters

MODIFIED CERCI THAT WORK LIKE FORCEPS

DARK STRIPES ON THE WINGS AND ABDOMEN

LONG ANTENNAE

TAN TO DARK BROWN BODY

Laugh Out Loud!

What do you get when you cross an earwig with a deep-sea fisherman?

A long shore earwig.

Black Webspinner

Oligotoma nigra ORDER **Embioptera**
• **LENGTH 0.35 in (9 mm)** • **HABITAT Underground
in leaf litter or in bark crevices on trees** • **RANGE
Southwestern United States from Texas to California
and as far north as Utah** • **Incomplete metamorphosis**

The Black Webspinner belongs
to the order Embioptera.
Insects in this order have small,
soft bodies and can spin webs out
of silk secreted from glands in their
forelegs. Both nymphs and adults are
able to do this. The Black Webspinner uses
this adaptation to spin silk tunnels under
leaves, in cracks in the bark on trees, and
under rocks. It lives in the silk tunnel, where it
is safe from predators. After nymphs hatch,
they spin and attach their own tunnels, creating a silk network for the family. It is believed
that Black Webspinners were accidentally
introduced to the United States on a shipment
of dates from Egypt in the late 1800s.

INSECT inspector!

Black Webspinner bodies
have adapted to live in narrow
silk tunnels. They have long,
slender bodies and their
strong rear muscles allow
them to move backward
quickly. Males have long oval
wings that also help with
backward movement. Females
have no wings.

MALE HAS OVAL WINGS.

SILK GLANDS IN FORELEGS

(FEMALE BODY IS REDDISH,
WITH NO WINGS)

10s spotters

Laugh Out Loud!
What's a webspinner's favorite vegetable?

Spin-ach!

SLANTED HEAD WITH THREE LONGITUDINAL RIDGES

Velvet-striped Grasshopper

Eritettix simplex ORDER **Orthoptera** ▪ LENGTH **0.6–0.9 in (15–23 mm)**
▪ HABITAT **Grassy hillsides and areas of dense vegetation** ▪ RANGE **South central Canada, east to Connecticut and south to New Mexico**
▪ Incomplete metamorphosis

10s spotters

BROWN BODY WITH GREEN MARKINGS

LONG WINGS EXTEND BEYOND ABDOMEN.

The Velvet-striped Grasshopper has a slanted face, a common characteristic among grasshoppers that specialize in eating grass. This species, which can be heard chirping throughout the day, comes in two color variations. It may be tan with brown markings or brown with green makings on its body. Long wings help the Velvet-striped Grasshopper evade predators. It can fly as far as 6 feet (1.8 m) at heights up to 12 inches (30.5 cm) off the ground. Velvet-striped Grasshoppers live in the Great Plains and also the Appalachian Mountains and their eastern slopes.

······································

BROWN COMPOUND EYE

10s spotters

Two-striped Grasshopper

Melanoplus bivittatus ORDER **Orthoptera** ▪ LENGTH **1.2–2 in (30.5–51 mm)** ▪ HABITAT **Tall grass prairie, wet meadows, roadsides, ditch banks, and crop borders** ▪ RANGE **Throughout the United States except southern Texas and the far Southeast; all but the far north in Canada** ▪ Incomplete metamorphosis

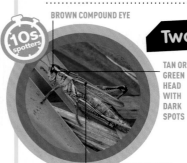

TAN OR GREEN HEAD WITH DARK SPOTS

TWO YELLOW STRIPES ALONG BODY

INSECT inspector!

The eggs of a Two-striped Grasshopper start developing during the summer. By the time winter comes, they are between 60 and 80 percent mature. They finish developing when soil temperatures rise. Because of the head start it got the previous summer, the Two-striped Grasshopper is one of the first species of grasshoppers to appear in the spring.

The Two-striped Grasshopper is a spur-throated grasshopper. It eats plants with broad, flat leaves and soft green stems. This grasshopper does not chirp. Its common name refers to the two pale yellow stripes that run along its back. Starting at the eyes, they extend to the tips of the wings. This big grasshopper can be found just about everywhere in the United States and throughout much of Canada. Both adults and nymphs migrate. Adults can fly 1,400 feet (427 m) above the ground.

Kiowa Grasshopper

Trachyrhachys kiowa **ORDER Orthoptera**
• **LENGTH 0.8–1.2 in (20.5–30.5 mm)** • **HABITAT Sparse**
grasslands dominated by short grasses • **RANGE**
Southwestern Canada through the United States,
except the Southeast; south to Guatemala
• **Incomplete metamorphosis**

The Kiowa Grasshopper is a banded-wing grasshopper. These hoppers may eat grasses or broad-leafed herbaceous plants, but the Kiowa Grasshopper prefers grasses and sedges. It is a big-headed, ground-dwelling insect. The Kiowa Grasshopper is highly responsive to changes in temperature and light. It rests horizontally on the ground at night. Soon after sunrise, it aligns its body perpendicular to the sun's rays, lowers the hind leg on the sunny side, and lets the sun shine on its exposed abdomen. As it gets hotter, the grasshopper climbs grasses and begins to feed. When it cools off, the grasshopper climbs back down. At sunset, it basks in the sun once again.

DARK NARROW BAND ON THE FRONT PART OF THE HEAD

NEARLY VERTICAL FACE

TAN BODY WITH DARK BROWN MARKINGS
(SOME ARE PALE GREEN WITH DARK MARKINGS.)

FRINGE HAIRS ON THE LOWER PART OF THE FEMUR

10s spotters

→ LISTEN FOR THIS
MALE BANDED-WING grasshoppers make a loud snapping, cracking, or buzzing sound when they fly. Females sometimes do, too. This happens because they rub the under surface of their forewings against the veins of their hind wings when they fly.

Laugh Out Loud!

Why did the grasshopper look out of place on his new team?

They were playing cricket!

Eastern Lubber Grasshopper

Romalea microptera ORDER **Orthoptera**
• LENGTH **2.4–3.1 in (61–78.5 mm)** • HABITAT **Open pine woods, weedy fields, and weedy vegetation along roadsides** • RANGE **Southeastern and south central United States** • **Incomplete metamorphosis**

Forget flying. The Eastern Lubber Grasshopper's wings are too short. Forget hopping. This slow, clumsy insect can only jump short distances. You're more likely to see it walking or crawling along. And depending on which stage of the life cycle you observe, this insect can have a vastly different appearance. Females produce an average of 60 eggs per egg pod. Those eggs hatch into completely black nymphs that have a bright yellow, orange, or red stripe on their backs. As the nymphs mature, the bright colors start to dominate. Adults are generally a dull yellow with black spots and markings but can also be black like the nymphs.

True or False

Q: The Eastern Lubber Grasshopper got its name because of its many colors.
A: False. It got its name for where it lives—eastern North America—and how it moves. *Lubber* comes from the Old English word *lobre,* which means "lazy" or "clumsy."

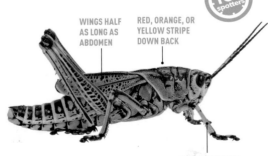

WINGS HALF AS LONG AS ABDOMEN

RED, ORANGE, OR YELLOW STRIPE DOWN BACK

LEGS ALLOW IT TO CRAWL, NOT HOP.

In the insect world, bright colors like those on the Eastern Lubber Grasshopper are a warning to stay away. When bright colors don't work, this grasshopper has other weapons to use against predators. It shoots out a foul-smelling, foul-tasting foam from its thorax, and it can make a loud hissing sound that scares animals away.

Black-sided Pygmy Grasshopper

Tettigidea lateralis **ORDER Orthoptera**
° **LENGTH 0.3–0.5 in (7.5–12.5 mm)** ° **HABITAT Moist environments, such as the shores of lakes and streams** ° **RANGE Eastern United States through the Great Plains, south into Central America**
° **Incomplete metamorphosis**

The Black-sided Pygmy Grasshopper, like all members of the family Tetrigidae, is small. Males grow up to 0.4 inch (10 mm), while females get just a bit larger. No tetrigid is longer than 0.8 inch (20 mm), or about the length of the sharpened end of a pencil. This grasshopper is dark brown. Some have a pale spot on the back femur. Others have a dark X on their backs. Males have a creamy yellow stripe on the lower part of their heads. The only thing big about it is its pronotum, or the plate-like structure that covers all or part of the thorax. It's nearly as long as the tiny hopper's abdomen.

INSECT inspector!

Pygmy grasshoppers are very hard to see. Their small size and coloration helps them blend in well with the environment. They're even harder to catch because they're strong, quick jumpers that hop around kind of like a flea! They'll even jump into the water to avoid being caught by a predator.

MAY HAVE DARK X ON BACK.

10S. spotters

ELONGATED PRONOTUM

PALE SPOT ON BACK FEMUR (POSSIBLE)

MALES HAVE CREAMY YELLOW STRIPE ON LOWER PART OF HEAD.

Pygmy Mole Cricket

Ellipes minuta **ORDER Orthoptera** • **LENGTH 0.15–0.24 in (4–6 mm)** • **HABITAT Sandy areas along rivers** • **RANGE Eastern United States, Midwest, south to Texas** • Incomplete metamorphosis

Names can be confusing, especially when you're trying to understand the "Pygmy" Mole Cricket. The words "pygmy" and "mole" make sense. This is a tiny insect that burrows its home in the ground. But the word "cricket" is confusing. After all, this little insect is more closely related to a grasshopper. Like its hopper cousins, the Pygmy Mole Cricket has extra-long back legs. These legs are so big that they're useless for walking. But they're great for jumping. On land, this little insect can jump as far as 3.3 feet (1 m) and as high as 2.3 feet (0.7 m). On water, the back legs turn into spring-loaded paddles. They push balls of water down, launching the Pygmy Mole Cricket as far as 1.3 inches (33 mm) and up to 3.9 inches (99 mm) high.

SHINY DARK OR BLACK COLOR

LARGE, FLATTENED BACK LEGS

10s spotters

Laugh Out Loud!

What did the little grasshopper holler when the class picked teams?

Pyg-my! Pyg-my!

Southern Wood Cricket

Gryllus fultoni **ORDER Orthoptera • LENGTH 0.6–1.2 in (15–30.5 mm) • HABITAT Upland pine, oak, and moist to dry broadleaf forests • RANGE Southeastern United States, except southern Florida** • Incomplete metamorphosis

The Southern Wood Cricket is the most widely distributed field cricket in the United States. All field crickets look similar. They have large, dark bodies with slight variations. And they usually are found on the ground. Until 1957, people thought there was only one species in the United States. Then biologists started to listen to the crickets' songs. The forewings of male field crickets are specialized to make sounds, and each species of cricket plays a different tune. The Southern Wood Cricket's song has about two fast-pulsed chirps per second.

BLACK BODY

BROWNISH BLACK LEGS

House Cricket

THREE DARK BANDS ON THE TOP OF THE HEAD AND BETWEEN THE EYES

Acheta domesticus **ORDER Orthoptera • LENGTH 0.6–0.8 in (15–20.5 mm) • HABITAT Grassy areas, woods, buildings and homes • RANGE Eastern United States, except southern Florida; Southern California** • Incomplete metamorphosis

Most likely native to southwestern Asia, the House Cricket is now found worldwide. It lives outdoors and can be found in grassy areas, along road-sides, and even around garbage dumps. Crickets are nocturnal, and they are attracted to lights. If a House Cricket makes its way into your home, you'll know. Like all crickets, it chirps. House Crickets eat plant material and dead or weakened insects. They'll also eat fabrics such as silk or wool. House Crickets are commonly sold for fish bait or as pet food.

LIGHT-YELLOWISH BROWN BODY

WINGS COVER THE ABDOMEN.

Snowy Tree Cricket

Oecanthus fultoni ORDER **Orthoptera** • LENGTH **0.6–0.7 in (15–18 mm)** • HABITAT **Shrubs and vines around homes, unsprayed fruit trees, neglected fence rows, scrubby oak trees** • RANGE **Throughout the United States, except the South and far northern regions** • Incomplete metamorphosis

ORANGE COLORING AND SMALL BLACK DOTS ON ITS HEAD

PALE GREEN TRANSLUCENT LEGS

INSECT inspector!

Scientists think that Snowy Tree Crickets chirp faster west of the Great Plains because they share their habitat with Riley's Tree Crickets, which are slow chirpers. Snowy Tree Crickets adapted to have a faster chirp so males can distinguish their sounds from those of the other species.

If you want to know how hot it is outside from July to November, listen for the Snowy Tree Cricket. This little cricket is also called the "thermometer cricket." The rate of its chirps changes with the temperature. In the eastern United States, count how many times the cricket chirps in 13 seconds. Then add 40. The answer will be very close to the current temperature. This works in the western United States, too. But crickets there chirp faster, so count the chirps for 12.5 seconds and add 38.

YELLOWISH GREEN BODY

Four-spotted Tree Cricket

Oecanthus quadripunctatus ORDER **Orthoptera** • LENGTH **0.5–0.6 in (12.5–15 mm)** • HABITAT **Open areas, including roadsides, oil fields, and crops** • RANGE **Throughout the United States** • Incomplete metamorphosis

The Four-spotted Tree Cricket has a pale, yellowish green body. It is named for the four spots at the base of its antennae. Unlike other tree crickets, the Four-spotted Tree Cricket is diurnal. It can often be heard singing at midday. Its call, which has been described as a continuous, shrill whistle, is hard to miss. The sound can go on for several minutes without stopping. On cold nights, the pitch drops and the sound becomes very faint. Four-spotted Tree Crickets prefer to live in fields filled with medium-size weeds.

FOUR SPOTS AT BASE OF ANTENNAE

YELLOW HEAD STREAKED WITH GREEN

Black-sided Camel Cricket

Ceuthophilus latens **ORDER Orthoptera**
• **LENGTH 0.5–0.6 in (12.5–15 mm)** • **HABITAT
Under flat rocks and logs in open area of
deciduous forests** • **RANGE Eastern United
States, Midwest, south to Texas**
• Incomplete metamorphosis

The Black-sided Camel
Cricket lays its eggs
underground. When the
eggs hatch, nymphs
emerge. They are yellowish
brown and have black bands
down each side, just like the adults.
This cricket has extra-long hind legs and
antennae that are three times as long as its
body. Those antennae are one of its main sensory organs. It uses them to communicate.
Being nocturnal, the Black-sided Camel Cricket
avoids light and is rarely seen during the day.
If you do spot one, it won't be far from a
nearby flat rock or log. These crickets can't
fly, so they don't stray too far from home.

Camel crickets are scavengers. They eat all sorts of
decaying organic material,
including dead insects,
mushrooms, and flowers.
Females will also eat the
males and nymphs if they
can't find anything else to
feed on.

10s spotters

EXTRA-LONG
HIND LEGS

BEIGE LEGS WITH
ROWS OF DARK
BROWN SPOTS

ARCHED BACK

BEIGE BODY

**Laugh
Out Loud!**

What is a Black-sided Camel Cricket's
favorite day of the week?

Hump Day!

LONG ANTENNAE

LEAF-GREEN BODY   **VEINED, OVAL WINGS**

True Katydid

Pterophylla camellifolia ORDER Orthoptera • LENGTH 1.5–2 in (38–51 mm) • HABITAT Deciduous trees in forests, woodlots, and yards • RANGE Southern New England to northern Florida and west to Iowa and eastern Texas • Incomplete metamorphosis

The True Katydid is the perfect example of mimicry. Its oval green wings have a veined, leathery texture. They look just like leaves. True Katydids spend most of their time in treetops. They are usually heard and not seen. Unlike their cousins the grasshoppers and crickets, both male and female True Katydids rub their right forewing across a set of teeth on the underside of the left forewing to sing. When one starts to call, others join in. On summer nights, you can hear them singing in a chorus that sounds like "Ka-ty-did, she-didn't, she did."

CONE-SHAPED HEAD

GREEN OR BROWN BODY (ADULTS HAVE LONG, NARROW FOREWINGS.)

Robust Conehead

Neoconocephalus robustus ORDER Orthoptera • LENGTH 2.1–2.9 in (53.5–73.5 mm) • HABITAT Moist upland prairies, cornfields, wet areas behind coastal dunes, and the edges of salt marshes • RANGE Eastern half of United States except far northern sections and Florida peninsula • Incomplete metamorphosis

The Robust Conehead produces a loud, continuous buzz with the intensity of 116 decibels. That's louder than a lawnmower or a jackhammer! Up close, it sounds like a low-pitched hum. Farther away, it's more like a whine. And if conditions are just right, the sound travels up to a third of a mile (500 m) away! Scientists think the high-pitched calls are defense against the echo-location of bats, a major katydid predator. Robust Coneheads may be brown or green. As the name suggests, their head is cone-shaped.

Laugh Out Loud!

How did the man know which insect ate all the leaves on his favorite tree?

He kept hearing, "Katy-did! Katy-did!"

Oblong-winged Katydid

10s. spotters

Amblycorypha oblongifolia ORDER **Orthoptera**
• LENGTH **1.6–2 in (40.5–51 mm)** • HABITAT **Edges of
saltwater marshes, in wet/dry meadows, shrubby fields,
and around forest edges** • RANGE **Eastern United States,
except most of Georgia and Florida; west to the Great Plains**
• Incomplete metamorphosis

The Oblong-winged Katydid is a
false katydid. This doesn't mean it's
not a real katydid. It just means the
noise it makes isn't like the traditional
katydid call. In this species, the call sounds
more like *itzic* or *zi-zit* instead of *ka-ty-did*,
ka-ty-did. The Oblong-winged Katydid's ears
are on its lower legs, just as the ears are on

**FULLY EXPOSED
"EAR" AT THE
BOTTOM OF
THE TIBIA**

**BROAD
FOREWINGS**

**COLORS CAN
BE PINK, ORANGE,
AND MORE.**

all katydids. Unlike other species, it comes in a rainbow of colors. It
may be pink, orange, tan, brown, or yellow. Originally, people thought
the colors were a response to the changing seasons. It turns out that
the colors are a genetically inherited condition.

**YELLOW STRIPE ON BACK OF
HEAD AND PROTHORAX**

Drumming Katydid

10s. spotters

Meconema thalassinum ORDER **Orthoptera** • LENGTH **0.6–0.7 in
(15–18 mm)** • HABITAT **Deciduous trees and surrounding vegetation**
• RANGE **Northeastern United States west to Michigan**
• Incomplete metamorphosis

PALE GREEN BODY

**TYMPANUM ON
EACH FRONT LEG**

Singing won't do for the Drumming
Katydid. Instead, males call to
females at night by rapidly tapping
one of their hind feet on leaves or
other ground surfaces. The drumming
is quiet, but sometimes it can be heard
up to 13 feet (4 m) away. The Drumming
Katydid is native to Europe. It most likely was
introduced to the United States as eggs on
woody ornamental plants. This insect lays its
eggs in the cracks and crevices in bark.

INSECT REPORT
MIGHTY MOUTHS

WHEN BUTTERFLIES ARE IN THE CATERPILLAR STAGE, THEY HAVE CHEWING MOUTHPARTS THAT HELP THEM EAT LEAVES. BUT WHEN THEY'RE ADULTS, THEY HAVE A LONG, HOLLOW PROBOSCIS. THE PROBOSCIS WORKS LIKE A SYPHON. THE BUTTERFLIES INSERT IT INTO FLOWERS AND SUCK OUT THE NECTAR. WHEN THEY'RE DONE DRINKING, THE PROBOSCIS COILS BACK UP.

Insects eat many different types of foods. Not all foods can be eaten in the same way. Because of that, the form and function of an insect's mouthparts match what it eats. Some insects, especially those that go through complete metamorphosis, change their diets as they move from one stage of development to the next. Their mouthparts change, too.

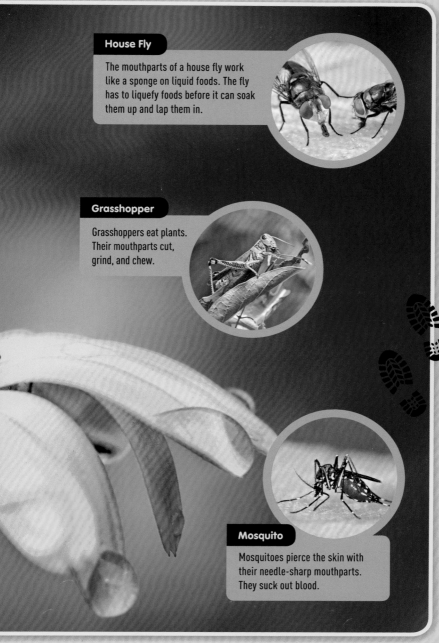

House Fly

The mouthparts of a house fly work like a sponge on liquid foods. The fly has to liquefy foods before it can soak them up and lap them in.

Grasshopper

Grasshoppers eat plants. Their mouthparts cut, grind, and chew.

Mosquito

Mosquitoes pierce the skin with their needle-sharp mouthparts. They suck out blood.

Webbing Barklouse

Archipsocus nomas ORDER **Psocodea**
• **LENGTH** Less than 0.13 in (3.5 mm) • **HABITAT** Smooth-barked shrubs and trees, young oaks, a variety of hardwood ornamental plants • **RANGE** Along the U.S. Gulf Coast from Texas to Florida and along the Atlantic coast north to South Carolina • Incomplete metamorphosis

Every year, certain types of trees along the Gulf Coast and southern Atlantic coast have tiny brown insects called Webbing Barklice living on them. But you won't notice these barklice until their population gets really high, which usually happens after a long period of humid weather. These insects spin silken webs. If enough Webbing Barklice get together, their webs can quickly cover the trunk, branches, and exposed roots of trees. Their webs don't cover the leaves, and they don't harm the trees. Neither do the barklice. They use their chewing mouthparts to feed on fungi, algae, and dead plant material on trees—not the trees themselves.

True or False

**Q: Scientists think Webbing Barklice spin webs to protect themselves from predators.
A: True**

**Q: Barklice are beneficial insects.
A: True.** They eat many undesirable inhabitants that live on tree bark.

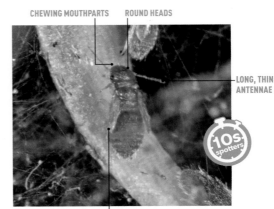

CHEWING MOUTHPARTS   ROUND HEADS

LONG, THIN ANTENNAE

TWO PAIRS OF MEMBRANOUS WINGS

Barklice are small, soft-bodied insects that act a bit like aphids. They are not lice. They are not parasitic. And they are not a pest to the trees and plants they live on. Webbing barklouse nymphs don't have wings, but adults do. They hold their wings above their bodies like a roof.

Veined Barklouse

Cerastipsocus venosus ORDER **Psocodea**
• LENGTH **About 0.25 in (6.5 mm)** • HABITAT **Trunks and branches of broadleaf trees and conifers, particularly maples and box elders** • RANGE **Quebec and Maine south to Florida, west to Texas and Minnesota, parts of Mexico** • Incomplete metamorphosis

Most of the time, Veined Barklice live under the radar in tree litter and under loose tree bark. But they're hard to miss when a bunch of nymphs and adults get together. Veined Barklice move around like a herd, a behavior that has earned them the nickname "tree cattle." Like all barklice, Veined Barklice have mouths built to chew. These scavengers eat fungi, algae, dead bark, and other materials on the trunks and larger limbs of trees. They don't eat leaves, and they don't bore into the trees. Veined Barklice are typically visible from May to October but can be seen year-round in southern states.

INSECT inspector!

Veined Barklice undergo incomplete metamorphosis. When nymphs hatch, they are wingless and have dark gray bodies with pale yellow bands between their abdominal segments. Adults have shiny black wings. Several hundred nymphs and adults can live together on one colony.

10s. spotters

CHEWING MOUTHPARTS

ROUND HEADS

LONG, THIN ANTENNAE

TWO PAIRS OF MEMBRANOUS WINGS

Laugh Out Loud! Why did the teacher make the barklice stay after school?

Its metamorphosis was incomplete!

Booklouse

Liposcelis corrodens ORDER **Psocodea**
- LENGTH **About 0.04 in (1 mm)** • HABITAT **Inside stored flour and grains, cereals, old books, and papers**
- RANGE **Throughout the United States; worldwide**
- Incomplete metamorphosis

Booklice are a group of tiny insects that can cause a lot of damage. The species *Liposcelis corrodens* is one of the most destructive of all. While many book-lice feast on bark and leaves, this tiny pest is common in flour mills and grain storage facilities. It can invade the cereal you eat for breakfast. You might also find it in a stack of old papers or inside a book. The food of choice of *Liposcelis corrodens* makes it a major pest in museums, too, where it will eat insect collections. Despite their name, these insects are not parasitic lice. They just have a louse-like appearance.

INSECT inspector!

All booklice are females. Nymphs grow inside unfertil-ized eggs. On average, one female lays about 60 eggs over her lifetime. Depending on environmental conditions, a booklouse can live between four weeks and two months.

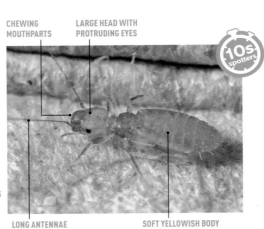

CHEWING MOUTHPARTS

LARGE HEAD WITH PROTRUDING EYES

10s spotters

WINGLESS

LONG ANTENNAE

SOFT YELLOWISH BODY

Laugh Out Loud!

Why did the school switch to an online library?

The booklice kept devouring the stories!

Head Louse

Pediculus humanus capitis **ORDER Phthiraptera** • **LENGTH 0.08–0.12 in (2–3 mm)** • **HABITAT Most commonly on the heads of preschool and elementary school-age children, their families and caretakers** • **RANGE Throughout the United States; worldwide** • **Incomplete metamorphosis**

 Whether you've had them or not, Head Lice are no stranger to school-age children. These tiny parasites are commonly passed from one person to another in schools, homes, or anywhere else children gather to play. The adult female attaches eggs, called nits, at the bottom of the hair shaft close to the scalp. The eggs hatch about a week later. Nymphs, which are about the size of a pin-head, take just one week to become adults. The sesame-seed-size adults have six clawed legs and tan to grayish white bodies. They can live on a person's head up to 30 days, sucking blood several times a day.

An estimated 6 million to 12 million children between the ages of 3 and 11 become infested with Head Lice each year in the United States. The claws of the Head Lice species found most commonly in the United States are better adapted to grab onto some types of hair than others. This could be why African Americans are less likely to have Head Lice than are people of other races.

SHORT ANTENNAE
SUCKING MOUTHPARTS
CONE-SHAPED HEAD

ONE LARGE CLAW ON EACH LEG

Laugh Out Loud! Why was the Head Louse happy when school started?

It was itching to make new friends.

Chicken Body Louse

Menacanthus stramineus **ORDER Phthiraptera**
• **LENGTH 0.12–0.14 in (3–3.5 mm)** • **HABITAT On chickens, particularly in large buildings with many chickens**
• **RANGE Throughout the United States; worldwide**
• **Incomplete metamorphosis**

The Chicken Body Louse infests chickens. These small, flat, wing-less parasites have mouthparts designed to chew instead of suck. They feed upon dry skin scales, scab tissue, and parts of the feathers. Once the female deposits eggs, it takes 4 to 7 days for them to hatch. In another 10 to 15 days, they become adults. An adult louse can live for about three weeks. It can lay between 50 to 300 eggs during that time. Biting lice don't usually spread diseases. In chickens they can cause severe skin irritation and weight loss. It can also make them lay fewer eggs.

True **or** False

Q: Lice spend their entire lives on an animal host.
A: True

Q: Some lice live in the ocean.
A: True. Members of the family Echinophthiriidae live on sea animals, including seals and sea lions.

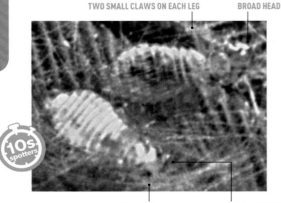

TWO SMALL CLAWS ON EACH LEG   BROAD HEAD

BITING MOUTHPARTS   SHORT ANTENNA

INSECT inspector!

Lice are parasitic insects. To survive, they must live, feed, and reproduce on the body of a living host. But they're still picky eaters. Typically, one type of louse will only affect one type of host. That means that Chicken Body Lice can't spread to a parakeet, blue jay, or robin. You can't get them, either.

Western Flower Thrips

Frankliniella occidentalis ORDER
Thysanoptera • LENGTH 0.04–0.09 in (1–2 mm)
• HABITAT Fields of crops or flowers, gardens, inside
greenhouses • RANGE Throughout North America
• Incomplete metamorphosis

The Western Flower Thrips is
a small, slender, winged insect
with a yellow to light brown
body. Females insert eggs into
the leaves or soft petal tissues on
a plant. This makes the eggs very
hard to see. After the eggs hatch, the larvae and adults are voracious eaters, feeding on
flowers, buds, terminals, leaves, and fruit. They
puncture plant cells with their mandibles and
suck up the cell contents. This causes leaves to
wither and die and flowers to be spotted and
deformed. Many buds don't even open. Although
native to western North America, it can now be
found everywhere thanks to the worldwide sell-
ing of trees and plants.

→ **LOOK FOR THIS**
**THE WESTERN FLOWER
THRIPS** damages plants
directly when it feeds on
various plant parts. It
causes even more damage
indirectly. Adults that fed
on infected plant tissue
as larvae transfer those
diseases to other plants.

10s spotters

NARROW FRINGED WINGS

PUNCHING-SUCKING MANDIBLE

(MALES: NARROW ABDOMEN)

FEMALES: ROUNDED ABDOMEN

INSECT inspector!

Western Flower Thrips feed on hundreds of different types of plants. They eat weeds, grass, fruits, and
vegetables. They also attack just about every type of plant that grows in a greenhouse.

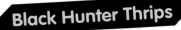

Black Hunter Thrips

Leptothrips mali ORDER **Thysanoptera**
• LENGTH **0.07 in (2 mm)** • HABITAT **Fruit trees** • RANGE
eastern North America • Incomplete metamorphosis

While many thrips are pests, others—like the Black Hunter—are valued predators. Normally found on deciduous fruit trees, the adult Black Hunter has a slender body with a sharply pointed abdomen. It is bluish black with silvery white wings. And it preys on everything from mites and aphids to leafhoppers and other thrips. When Black Hunters feed, they don't injure the plant. They're team players, too, getting along well with other predatory species. But even though the Black Hunter is a very active predator, its effectiveness is limited. Females don't lay many eggs. This makes it hard for the population of these insects to grow very quickly.

SILVERY WHITE WINGS

SLENDER, SHARPLY POINTED BODY

Laugh Out Loud!

How did the little Black Hunter scrape its knee?

It thripped!

17-year Cicada

Magicicada septendecim ORDER **Hemiptera** • LENGTH **1.5 in (38 mm)** • HABITAT **Deciduous forests** • RANGE **Northern Midwest and eastern United States** • Incomplete metamorphosis

The 17-year Cicada is a periodical cicada, or one that emerges as a mass brood after a period of years. This mob behavior likely helps the cicadas overwhelm predators. It's also essential for reproduction. Females mature and lay eggs in the twigs of trees. Nymphs hatch and burrow underground. They stay there for 17 years, feeding off the roots of deciduous trees. In the spring of the 17th year, just like clockwork, the entire brood makes its way to the surface. Nymphs go through one final molt to become very noisy adults.

SUCKING MOUTHPARTS, LIKE A SMALL, SHARP STRAW

REDDISH ORANGE EYES AND LEGS

CLEAR WINGS WITH ORANGE VEINS

BLACK BODY

SUCKING MOUTHPARTS, LIKE A SMALL, SHARP STRAW

BLACK EYES

Dog Day Cicada

Tibicen canicularis ORDER **Hemiptera** • LENGTH **Up to 2 in (51 mm)** • HABITAT **Mixed or deciduous forests** • RANGE **Northern United States and southern Canada**

Even though they have two-year life cycles, most of which is spent underground, Dog Day Cicadas are classified as annual cicadas. That's because different broods emerge each year. Dog Day Cicadas have tan or brown wingless nymphs. The camouflage-colored adults rarely fly far from trees. Their sound travels much farther. Cicadas have a pair of drumskin-like organs at the base of their abdomen. They vibrate those organs at a high speed, creating a buzzing sound. This cicada's loud, continuous buzz gets louder and louder for about a minute before it peaks and dies back down.

10s spotters

BLACK, GREEN, OR OLIVE CAMOUFLAGE-PATTERNED BODIES

FOUR MEMBRANOUS WINGS

PIERCING MOUTHPARTS

USUALLY GREEN ON TOP

TAN TO DARK BROWN LEGS AND UNDERSIDE

Grass Sharpshooter

Draeculacephala minerva ORDER **Hemiptera** ∙ LENGTH **0.25–0.36 in (6.5–9 mm)** ∙ HABITAT **Perennial grass areas that are regularly irrigated** ∙ RANGE **West Coast, southwestern United States, Florida, Hawaii, Massachusetts, and south into Mexico** ∙ Incomplete metamorphosis

Perennial grasses are the favorite meal of the Grass Sharpshooter. Like other leafhoppers, the Grass Sharpshooter has piercing mouthparts that it uses like a tap to suck all the sap out of the xylem and phloem of plant tissues. If the population gets large enough, it can cause a lot of damage. Green grass turns gray and then yellow. People often think the damage is the result of drought. Three generations of Grass Sharpshooters can grow within one year. Nymphs are brown. Adults born in summer months are bright green. Those born in the fall have a dull brown color.

GRAYISH YELLOW BODY WITH DARK BROWN MARKINGS

Gray Lawn Leafhopper

Exitianus exitiosus ORDER **Hemiptera** ∙ LENGTH **0.06–0.13 in (1.5–3 mm)** ∙ HABITAT **Lawns, particularly those with Bermuda grass** ∙ RANGE **Throughout the United States, southern Canada, and northern Mexico** ∙ Incomplete metamorphosis

TWO BLACK SPOTS ON BACK OF HEAD

CLEAR TO WHITE WINGS WITH BROWN VEINS

The Gray Lawn Leafhopper is another plant vampire that uses its piercing mouthparts to suck the juices out of plants. This little insect's favorite meal is your front lawn! Unfortunately, when it feeds on your grass it can also transmit damaging viruses. The Gray Lawn Leafhopper is native to the United States. For good reason, it's also considered to be a major pest. If you disturb leafhoppers in your yard, you'll see that they are true acrobats. Leafhoppers are great fliers. They can also hop forward, backward, or sideways like a crab.

Pea Aphid

Acyrthosiphon pisum **ORDER Hemiptera** • **LENGTH 0.08–0.16 in (2–4 mm)** • **HABITAT Wherever peas and alfalfa are grown** • **RANGE Throughout the United States and Canada** • **Incomplete metamorphosis**

The Pea Aphid might be a huge agricultural pest, but it's also one very interesting insect. Tens of millions of years ago, this little sap-sucker got part of its DNA from fungi! Like plants, it can produce its own carotenoids. Carotenoids are the color pigments that make carrots orange. Pea Aphids use them to make their bodies green or pink, which is a handy adaptation to have when you want to avoid predators. Like plants, Pea Aphids might also be able to turn sunlight into energy to make their own food. Scientists aren't quite sure how this ability helps Pea Aphids. Their diet is already loaded with more sugar than they could ever use.

INSECT inspector!

Aphid populations can spread really quickly. Males mate with some of the females that have wings. Females that don't have wings can become pregnant all by themselves. So can the nymphs they're carrying. These baby insects are pregnant when they're born!

LONG, THIN LEGS AND ANTENNAE

NARROW DARK BAND AT TIP OF THIRD ANTENNAL SEGMENT

PEAR-SHAPED BODY GENERALLY GREEN, CAN BE PINK

10s spotters

Laugh Out Loud!

What musical instrument did the aphid want to learn how to play?

A phid-dle!

Harlequin Bugs

Harlequin Bugs are true bugs. True bugs only undergo incomplete metamorphosis, growing from an egg to a nymph to an adult.

WATER STRIDERS BELONG TO THE ORDER HEMIPTERA. THEY ARE TRUE BUGS.

People tend to think the words "insect" and "bug" mean the same thing. They don't. Insects are animals born from eggs. They have six legs, segmented bodies, and three main body parts. Bugs are just one type of insect. All true bugs belong to the order Hemiptera.

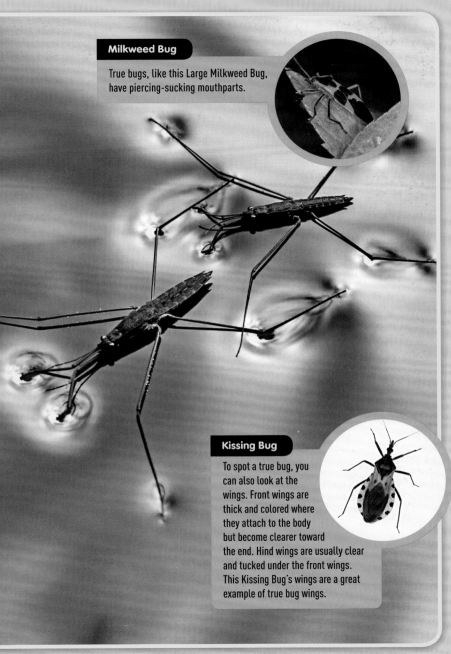

Milkweed Bug

True bugs, like this Large Milkweed Bug, have piercing-sucking mouthparts.

Kissing Bug

To spot a true bug, you can also look at the wings. Front wings are thick and colored where they attach to the body but become clearer toward the end. Hind wings are usually clear and tucked under the front wings. This Kissing Bug's wings are a great example of true bug wings.

Kissing Bug

Triatoma lecticularia ORDER **Hemiptera** • LENGTH **0.6–0.9 in (15–23 mm)** • HABITAT **In cracks and holes in buildings, under porches, rocks, cement, in animal burrows, in dog houses, etc.** • RANGE **Southern United States** • Incomplete metamorphosis

ORANGE-YELLOW MARKINGS EXTENDING HORIZONTALLY ON ABDOMINAL SEGMENTS

ORANGE-YELLOW LATERAL MARKINGS ON BODY

PIERCING-SUCKING MOUTHPARTS

Its name sounds sweet, but the Kissing Bug is one insect you're better off staying away from. Kissing Bugs are a type of assassin bug. They're bloodsucking pests that prey on anything with blood—including humans. Kissing Bugs hide in cracks and other tight places during the day. They usually feed at night and can feast for up to half an hour. After a meal, this bug will most likely scamper away. But if you happen to spot one of these hairy black and orange bugs in your bed, you may have just been bitten!

Wheel Bug

LONG ANTENNAE

SPINY RIDGE ON THORAX

Arilus cristatus ORDER **Hemiptera** • LENGTH **1–1.25 in (25.5–32 mm)** • HABITAT **Gardens, orchards, meadows, and open fields** • RANGE **Midwest and southeastern United States** • Incomplete metamorphosis

STOUT BEAK, PIERCING-SUCKING MOUTHPARTS

LONG LEGS

The Wheel Bug is a formidable sight. This grotesque-looking creature has long legs and antennae, a stout beak, and big eyes on its skinny head. It's also got a spiny ridge sticking up from its thorax that looks like a wheel. If that weren't enough, they stink, too! Wheel Bugs have a pair of bright orangish red scent sacs. When disturbed, they force those sacs to come out of their anus and release a pungent stench. Both nymphs, which lack the wheel, and adults are predators of caterpillars, beetles, aphids, and other soft-bodied insects.

Large Milkweed Bug

Oncopeltus fasciatus ORDER **Hemiptera**
• **LENGTH 0.35–0.7 in (9–18 mm)** • **HABITAT Fields and meadows that contain milkweed plants** • **RANGE Throughout North America, southern Canada, and Mexico** • **Incomplete metamorphosis**

It's easy to spot a Large Milkweed Bug. Both adults and nymphs have bright reddish orange and black patterns on their backs. These colors are a warning to predators. Not only does this bug taste bad, it's toxic when eaten, too! The Large Milkweed Bug feeds on the seeds of milkweed plants. It pokes its piercing mouthpart into the ripening seed, injects digestive enzymes, and sucks out the now liquefied food. In the process, it ingests toxic compounds contained within the seeds. These bugs undergo incomplete metamorphosis. They lay light-yellow eggs in cracks between milkweed pods. As the eggs develop, they turn red. Nymphs molt five times. Once this bug reaches adulthood, it lives for about a month.

INSECT inspector!

Large Milkweed Bugs migrate, just like another species that depends on the milkweed plant—the Monarch butterfly. They spend winters in southern states and Mexico and fly as far north as southern Canada in the summer.

10s spotters

PIERCING-SUCKING MOUTHPARTS

REDDISH ORANGE AND BLACK PATTERNS ON BACK

Laugh Out Loud!

Why did the teacher believe the seed bug when it told her the dog ate its homework?

It was a true bug.

Hairy Chinch Bug

Blissus leucopterus hirtus ORDER **Hemiptera** • LENGTH **0.12–0.16 in (3–4 mm)** • HABITAT **Cool-season turf grasses** • RANGE **Northern and northeastern United States, south to Virginia** • Incomplete metamorphosis

Hairy Chinch Bugs are another insect that can suck the sap right out of plants. They are the most destructive pest on northern lawns. Not only do these bugs rob grass of the fluids it needs to survive, but they also inject toxins when they pierce the crowns and stems of the blades with their pointed mouthparts. This causes the grass to wilt, turn yellow, turn brown, and then die. Hairy Chinch Bugs take shelter during winter as adults. They emerge in the spring and lay eggs once the temperature reaches 70°F (21°C). When nymphs hatch, they have reddish orange bodies with a white stripe on their backs. After a series of five molts, their bodies darken. Adults have black bodies with shiny white wings.

→ **LOOK FOR THIS**
HAIRY CHINCH BUGS may have long wings or short wings. Like all true bugs, their wings fold flat over their bodies. If the insect's wings are long, the tips of its wings overlap.

BLACK BODY

PIERCING-SUCKING MOUTHPARTS

WHITE WINGS

SMALL BLACK SPOT IN CENTER AREA OF EACH WING

Laugh Out Loud!

What do you call a large group of chinch bugs?

A chinch-a-lada!

Bed Bug

Cimex lectularius ORDER **Hemiptera**
LENGTH 0.24–0.37 in (6–9.5 mm) ▪ **HABITAT Human dwellings, bird nests, bat caves** ▪ **RANGE Throughout the United States; worldwide** ▪ Incomplete metamorphosis

 Bed Bugs are parasitic bugs found all over the world. By day they hide in tight places like in the seams along mattress edges. At night, they come out to feed, sucking blood from human hosts. It takes 5 to 10 minutes for the bug to get its fill of blood. As it does, its broad, flat, brown body swells up like a red blimp. Unlike some other parasitic bugs, Bed Bugs don't need a dirty environment to thrive. They do just as well in spotless homes and five-star hotels. They also don't need a meal every day. Nymphs can survive a couple of months between feedings. Adults can wait up to a year.

INSECT inspector!

When Bed Bugs bite, they inject the person with an anesthetic and a substance that keeps blood from clotting. Because of this, the person being bitten probably won't feel a thing.

LEATHERY, REDUCED FOREWINGS

BROAD, FLAT, OVAL-SHAPED BODY

SHORT, STIFF HAIRS ON SIDE OF PRONOTUM

PIERCING-SUCKING MOUTHPARTS

10s spotters

→ LOOK FOR THIS

BED BUGS can leave small bite marks, particularly on the face, neck, arms, and hands. Sometimes they don't leave any marks at all. And bite marks can take up to two weeks to show. If you start to itch, search for other signs of a problem. Search for Bed Bugs or their exoskeletons in your mattress or sheets. Look for rusty-colored blood spots on the sheets. Then use your nose. Bed Bugs have a sweet, musty odor.

Harlequin Bug

Murgantia histrionica **ORDER Hemiptera**
• **LENGTH 0.3–0.4 in (7.5–10 mm)** • **HABITAT Crops of cabbage and related plants** • **RANGE Southern United States** • Incomplete metamorphosis

A Harlequin Bug's life cycle begins as one of about a dozen little barrel-shaped eggs on the underside of a leaf. The eggs are white and have two black rings around them and one black spot in the middle. They hatch in 4 to 29 days. It all depends on the temperature. When nymphs are born, their bodies are orange and black. They go through five or six developmental stages before they become adults. This stink bug is not native to the United States. It invaded the southern states from Mexico shortly after the Civil War. It is now a major pest for some crops. Adults and nymphs kill plants when they suck the juices out of plant tissue.

INSECT inspector!

Adult Harlequin Bugs have bright red and black spotted bodies shaped like flat shields. Their forewings overlap on their backs. These bright colors warn predators to stay away. If predators don't listen and try to eat one of these bugs anyway, they're in for a surprise. Harlequin Bugs can create a stink. In addition, they have chemicals in their bodies that make them taste like spicy hot mustard!

RED AND BLACK SPOTTED BODY

10s spotters

PIERCING-SUCKING MOUTHPARTS

FLAT, SHIELD-SHAPED BODY

ODOROUS GLANDS ON ABDOMEN

Laugh Out Loud!

What did the judge say when the Harlequin Bug entered the courtroom?

"Odor in the court!"

Southern Green Stink Bug

Nezara viridula **ORDER Hemiptera** ▪ **LENGTH 0.5 –0.7 in (12.5–18 mm)** ▪ **HABITAT Ornamentals, weeds, citrus fruits, cultivated crops** ▪ **RANGE Southern United States** ▪ Incomplete metamorphosis

To spot a Southern Green Stink Bug in the United States, you'd have to go to the lower half of the country. But worldwide, this insect pest has a very wide range. Originally, it came from Ethiopia in Africa. Like all stink bugs, the Southern Green Stink Bug has a shield-shaped body. But as this bug's name suggests, the adult's body is solid green. Nymphs look very different. When first born, nymphs are light yellow. They have red eyes and transparent legs and antennae. As they grow, they turn red and black. Nymphs don't start to take on the adult's coloring until they've gone through five molts.

→ **LOOK FOR THIS**
ALL INSECTS HAVE a scutellum, which is a triangle-shaped part of the thorax. On a stink bug, that part is so large that it extends halfway down the back.

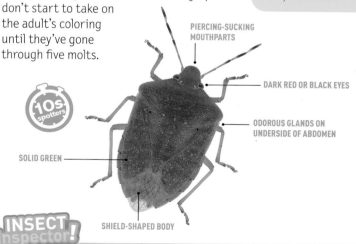

10s spotters

PIERCING-SUCKING MOUTHPARTS

DARK RED OR BLACK EYES

ODOROUS GLANDS ON UNDERSIDE OF ABDOMEN

SOLID GREEN

SHIELD-SHAPED BODY

INSECT inspector!

The Southern Green Stink Bug injects toxic saliva when it bites into a young green fruit. Cells at the feeding site die so that part of the fruit stops growing. The surrounding areas don't. Because of this, the fruit looks like it has dimples and is irregularly shaped. This effect is called catfacing.

Tarnished Plant Bug

Lygus lineolaris ORDER **Hemiptera** • LENGTH **0.5–0.7 in (12.5–18 mm)** • HABITAT **Temperate non-desert areas** • RANGE **Southern United States** • Incomplete metamorphosis

The Tarnished Plant Bug isn't picky when it comes to finding a meal. Adults feed on hundreds of different plant species, resulting in dimpled, catfaced fruits and short, bushy ornamental flowers. This true bug has a yellowish brown body with reddish brown markings on the wings. Eggs are hard to spot because females insert them into the tissue of weeds and grasses with just one short end exposed. Nymphs emerge from this end about a week after being laid. Tarnished Plant Bugs overwinter as adults. Two to three generations are born each year.

PIERCING-SUCKING MOUTHPARTS

LONG, OVAL, SOMEWHAT FLAT BODY

YELLOWISH BROWN BODY WITH RED MARKINGS

Four-lined Plant Bug

LIME GREEN BODY

Poecilocapsus lineatus ORDER **Hemiptera** • LENGTH **0.25–0.3 in (6.5–7.5 mm)** • HABITAT **Perennials and shrubs in urban landscapes** • RANGE **East of the Rocky Mountains** • Incomplete metamorphosis

The Four-lined Plant Bug, found east of the Rocky Mountains, is the most common plant bug found on perennials and landscape shrubs. These bugs overwinter as eggs. Both nymphs and adults pierce plant tissues with their mouthparts and suck out the liquefied tissues inside. This causes leaves to become distorted and curled. A hole can also appear at the injection site. Nymphs are wingless and have orange-red bodies. Adults are lime green and have four black stripes on their backs. Just one generation of Four-lined Plant Bugs is born each year.

FOUR BLACK STRIPES ON BACK

PIERCING-SUCKING MOUTHPARTS

Water Strider

Aquarius remigis **ORDER Hemiptera**
• **LENGTH 0.5–0.75 in (12.5–19 mm)** • **HABITAT Calm waters in freshwater areas** • **RANGE Throughout the United States and Canada** • Incomplete metamorphosis

If you've ever seen a bug that looked like it was walking on water, you were probably looking at a Water Strider. Like all insects, Water Striders have three pairs of legs. But this bug has tiny needle-shaped hairs on the ends of its long, spindly legs. Air gets trapped in the spaces between these hairs and forms an air cushion. The Water Strider floats on top of that cushion and its body never even gets wet. Water Striders are predators. If they feel ripples on the water's surface, they skate over to eat the unfortunate insect that accidentally fell in. They also eat mosquito larvae.

INSECT inspector!

Antennae are sensory organs. Water striders use them to feel their surroundings. But on males, the antennae have evolved into large, muscular devices with hooks and spikes. They help males hold onto females during mating.

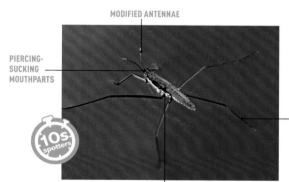

MODIFIED ANTENNAE

PIERCING-SUCKING MOUTHPARTS

LONG, SPINDLY LEGS COVERED WITH HAIRS

10s spotters

DARK BROWN, ELONGATED BODY

Laugh Out Loud! Why are Water Striders such easygoing bugs?

They take everything in stride.

Water Boatman

Sigara alternata **ORDER Hemiptera** • **LENGTH 0.24 in (6 mm)** • **HABITAT Still waters with aquatic plants, including ponds, lake edges, sewage tanks, birdbaths, and swimming pools** • **RANGE Eastern United States and Canada** • Incomplete metamorphosis

The Water Boatman is a great flier, but its body is definitely built for surviving in the water. It's light on bottom and dark on top. This coloring helps the bug blend into the environment and escape predators. In addition, the Water Boatman's body is shaped like a boat and its flat, hairy hind legs paddle like oars. This aquatic insect can also submerge. It wraps a bubble of air around its wings and abdomen. That bubble gives the bug oxygen to breathe, but it also makes it float toward the surface. Water Boatmen have to grab onto plants to pull themselves down into the water.

True or False

Q: Water Boatmen bite people.
A: **False**
....
Q: Some species of Water Boatmen live in the Himalaya.
A: **True.** And other species live in Death Valley!

SCOOP-LIKE FRONT LEGS   BODY: LIGHT UNDERNEATH/DARK ON TOP

10s spotters

PIERCING-SUCKING MOUTHPARTS   FLAT, HAIRY HIND LEGS

INSECT inspector!

The Water Boatman's hind legs are adapted for swimming. The front legs have a much different use. Males rub their front legs against their heads under the water. This creates a chirping sound that attracts mates.

Backswimmer

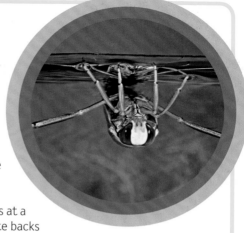

Notonecta unifasciata **ORDER Hemiptera**
LENGTH 0.39 in (10 mm) • **HABITAT Ponds, freshwater
pools, slow-flowing streams** • **RANGE Throughout
North America** • Incomplete metamorphosis

Backswimmers are aquatic insects that swim upside down through the water. They trap air in pockets at the tip of their abdomen. The air supply allows them to stay underwater for up to six hours at a time. Backswimmers have white backs and are dark underneath. This color combination helps them blend in with the environment. They also have three pairs of specialized legs. Their flat, hairy back legs work just like oars. They use their front legs to catch prey and their middle legs to hold it tight. They kill prey, mainly small fish and tadpoles, with their piercing mouthparts. Never pick up one of these bugs. Those mouthparts deliver a very painful bite!

DANGER!

A Backswimmer's bite can hurt as much as a bee sting. Because of this, some people call them "water wasps" or "water bees."

BODY: DARK ON TOP/LIGHT UNDERNEATH

PIERCING-SUCKING MOUTHPARTS

CLEAR WINGS

FLAT, HAIRY HIND LEGS

→ LOOK FOR THIS

THE BACKSWIMMER is often confused with another aquatic insect, the Water Boatman. To tell the difference, look at the coloring. Water Boatmen are dark on top and light on bottom. Backswimmers are the opposite. Then look at how the insect is swimming. If it's right side up, it's a Water Boatman. If it's upside down, it's a Backswimmer.

INSECT REPORT
INVASIVE SPECIES

PEOPLE ARE USUALLY RESPONSIBLE WHEN INVASIVE SPECIES ARE INTRODUCED INTO A NEW ENVIRONMENT. TINY INSECTS CAN EASILY HITCHHIKE IN WATER, WOODEN SHIPPING CRATES, AND SHIPMENTS OF ORNAMENTAL PLANTS.

People move from place to place. So do insects. And this isn't always good. Sometimes insects cause harm when they are accidentally introduced to new environments. They can crowd out native species, kill native plants, or even pose a threat to people living in the area.

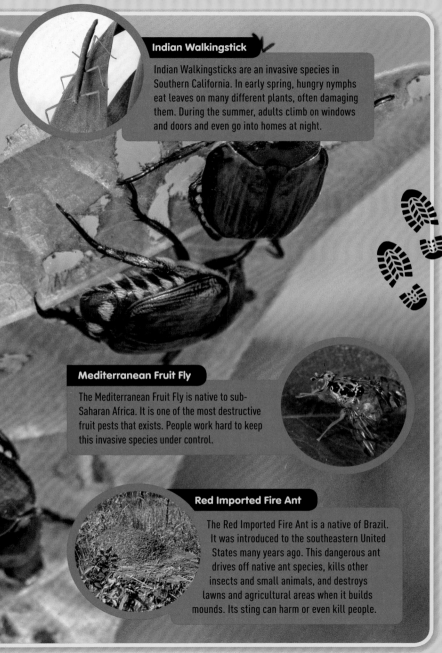

Indian Walkingstick

Indian Walkingsticks are an invasive species in Southern California. In early spring, hungry nymphs eat leaves on many different plants, often damaging them. During the summer, adults climb on windows and doors and even go into homes at night.

Mediterranean Fruit Fly

The Mediterranean Fruit Fly is native to sub-Saharan Africa. It is one of the most destructive fruit pests that exists. People work hard to keep this invasive species under control.

Red Imported Fire Ant

The Red Imported Fire Ant is a native of Brazil. It was introduced to the southeastern United States many years ago. This dangerous ant drives off native ant species, kills other insects and small animals, and destroys lawns and agricultural areas when it builds mounds. Its sting can harm or even kill people.

Golden-eyed Lacewing

Chrysopa oculata **ORDER Neuroptera**
• **LENGTH 0.39–0.79 in (10–20.5 mm)** • **HABITAT
Meadows with low vegetation, trees and field
crops** • **RANGE Throughout North America**
• Complete metamorphosis

The Golden-eyed Lacewing may look delicate, with its lightly veined, translucent wings. But this insect is one hungry predator. Adults have chewing mouthparts. At night, they search for pollen, nectar, and honeydew. Some adults eat small insects. Larvae, which look like mini alligators and have piercing mouthparts, search for any soft-bodied insect they can get. When larvae bite into an insect, they paralyze it with venom. Then they suck the fluids out of the insect's body. One larva can eat more than 200 aphids or other type of prey in just one week. To keep newly hatched larvae from eating each other, female lacewings lay eggs on short, slender stalks.

**→ LOOK FOR THIS
LACEWINGS** belong to the order Neuroptera. The name Neuroptera comes from the Greek words *neur*, which means "nerve," and *pter*, which means "wing." Insects in this order have clear wings. This makes it easy to see the netlike pattern of nerves on their wings.

BLACK BAND AT FRONT OF HEAD

TRANSLUCENT, VEINED WINGS

RED CIRCLES AROUND THE SECOND SEGMENT OF EACH LONG, SLENDER, LIGHT-GREEN ANTENNAE

INSECT inspector!

Lacewing adults have earned themselves a not so attractive name—stink flies! If you disturb a lacewing, it will send out a really stinky smell. Lacewings also release the stench to defend themselves against predators.

Antlion

Glenurus gratus ORDER **Neuroptera**
○ LENGTH **1.4–2.4 in (35.5–61 mm)** ○ HABITAT **Sandy dunes, hollow trees, forest floors, under hedges, and in dark, shady areas** ○ RANGE **Eastern United States**
○ Complete metamorphosis

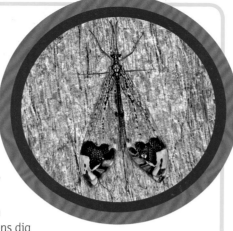

 Antlions have some pretty interesting nicknames—everything from "demons in the dust" to "doodlebugs." And it's all because of the show they put on while trying to catch prey. Antlions dig pits in the ground to trap ants. Only the best places will do, so these insects meander along searching for the perfect spot to dig. They leave a path that looks like an aimless doodle in their wake. Once an Antlion find the perfect spot, it spirals down until the pit is deep enough. Ants that fall into the pit are met with a pair of pincers armed with a poisonous stinger. One Antlion can devour about 22 ants in one day.

INSECT inspector!

Antlion larvae live in hollows of trees. They sit and wait for prey to approach. They trap prey with their curved, toothed mandibles, which work together to create a pair of sucking tubes.

10s spotter

TUBELIKE ABDOMEN

FOUR MEMBRANOUS WINGS WITH NETLIKE PATTERNS OF VEINS

DARK TIPS ON WINGS

Laugh Out Loud! What is the Antlion's favorite kind of cookie?

Snickerdoodles!

Green Mantidfly

Zeugomantispa minuta ORDER **Neuroptera** • LENGTH **0.59–0.79 in (15–20.5 mm)** • HABITAT **On leaves and stems where hunting spiders crawl** • RANGE **Eastern United States north to Pennsylvania and west to Texas, Illinois, and Wisconsin** • Complete metamorphosis

10s. spotters

The Green Mantidfly has raptor-like fore-legs in the front and transparent, veined wings in the back. It looks like a cross between a European Mantis (aka Praying Mantis) and a Green Lacewing. Females lay clusters of about 1,000 eggs. They attach eggs to leaves on short, transparent stalks. After larvae hatch, they hitch a ride on a spider to get to their favorite food—spider eggs. If they're lucky, the spider is a female and they can enter the egg sac to feast. If it's a male, they switch hosts when the spiders mate.

TRANSPARENT, VEINED WINGS

GREEN BODY

ELONGATED PROTHORAX AND RAPTOR-LIKE FORELEGS

....

CHEWING MOUTHPARTS

Wasp Mantidfly

Climaciella brunnea ORDER **Neuroptera** • LENGTH **1.7–1.85 in (43–47 mm)** • HABITAT **Established fields with flowers** • RANGE **Central and western United States, southern Canada** • Complete metamorphosis

10s. spotters

Wasp Mantidflies protect themselves by mimicking two more dangerous preda-tors. They have the raptor-like forelegs of a European Mantis (aka Praying Mantis) and the coloring and behaviors of a paper wasp. Wasp Mantidfly larvae feed on spider eggs. If eggs aren't avail-able, they'll suck blood out of a spider host. Adults eat a variety of small insects and drink nectar. They'll also eat each other. Adults use their wasplike characteristics to scare preda-tors away. If the coloring isn't enough, an adult will curl its abdomen into stinging position and spread its wings when threatened.

RAPTOR-LIKE FORELEGS AND ELONGATED PROTHORAX

BLACK AND BROWN BANDED ABDOMEN

Eastern Dobsonfly

Corydalus cornutus **ORDER Megaloptera**
• **LENGTH 2.95 in (75 mm)** • **HABITAT Near rivers and streams**
• **RANGE Eastern United States** • Complete metamorphosis

LARGE MANDIBLES

TAN OR LIGHT BROWN BODIES WITH DARKER MOTTLING

TWO PAIRS OF STRONGLY VEINED WINGS

The Eastern Dobsonfly is a large insect. Its body is about 3 inches (7.5 cm) long and its wings spread up to 5 inches (12.7 cm) wide. It can also be a bit scary to look at. Adults have sickle-shaped mandibles. The adult male's jaws can be up to an inch (2.5 cm) long. These jaws aren't strong. In fact, they're mostly for show. Their larvae, called hellgram-mites, are the top invertebrate predators in their rocky stream habitats. Because of their strong mandibles for eating, hellgrammites are sometimes called "toe-biters."

Spring Fishfly

TAN OR BEIGE BODY

Chauliodes rastricornis **ORDER Megaloptera** • **LENGTH 0.8–1.8 in (20.5–45.5 mm)** • **HABITAT Near rivers and streams** • **RANGE Northeast and upper Midwest United States** • Complete metamorphosis

LONG COMBED ANTENNAE

LARGE LACY WINGS

Spring Fishflies are nocturnal insects with tan or beige bodies, large lacy wings, and long combed antennae. They lack the powerful jaws found on their close cous-ins, the dobsonflies. Females lay masses of eggs on rocks, tree trunks, or leaves near still bodies of water. When the eggs hatch, larvae crawl into the nearest water source. Once the larvae get big enough, they crawl toward land and turn into pupae. Two weeks later, the pupae morph into adults. Adults live a few days, which is just enough time to lay eggs.

INSECT inspector!

The order Megaloptera includes dobsonflies, fishflies, and alderflies. These insects are recognized for their large wings. They're also considered to be some of the most ancient insects that undergo complete metamorphosis. The first Megaloptera appeared more than 259 million years ago.

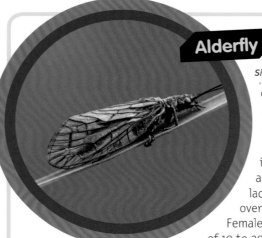

Alderfly

Sialis infumata ORDER **Megaloptera**
• LENGTH **0.4 in (10 mm)** • HABITAT **On vegetation near ponds and slow-moving streams** • RANGE **Throughout the United States, southwestern Canada** • Complete metamorphosis

Alderflies are dark brown insects with long, delicate antennae. They fold their lacy veined wings like a roof over their backs when at rest. Females lay multiple eggs in rows of 10 to 20 eggs each under bridges or on plants overhanging water. This allows newly hatched larvae to simply fall into the water. They live here for the next year or two, feeding on small mayflies and midges. When larvae are ready, they crawl to land to become pupae that transform into adults. Alderfly adults do not eat during their short lives. All attention is given to mating and laying eggs. Unlike their nocturnal relatives, dobsonflies and fishflies, alderflies are active during the day.

True or False

Q: Alderfly larvae have gills.
A: True. The larvae live in water. They use the gills along the sides of their abdomens to breathe.

Q: Alderflies are strong fliers.
A: False. They're actually pretty clumsy in the air.

TWO PAIRS OF MEMBRANOUS WINGS

CHEWING MOUTHPARTS

LONG ANTENNAE

LONG, SOFT, FLEXIBLE BODY

10s. spotters

Laugh Out Loud! How do alderfly eggs like to pass the time?

Hanging out with their friends.

Snakefly

Raphidia bicolor **ORDER Raphidioptera**
• **LENGTH 0.59–0.87 in (15–22 mm)** • **HABITAT Forests
and shrubs** • **RANGE Western United States and
southwestern Canada** • Complete metamorphosis

Appearance—and not
behavior—explains why the
Snakefly is named after a
snake. Adults have an elongated prothorax, or neck, and a
small head, which makes this insect
resemble a snake. Snakeflies are
brown, flying insects that live in the western half of the United States. At just over
half an inch (15 mm) long, they're not huge.
But they are extremely beneficial to have
around. Larvae live on bark and in soil. With
their chewing mouthparts, they eat grubs
and other insects that can kill plants. Adults
prefer to feast on aphids, which cause
damage to a wide variety of host plants.

Snakeflies are known for
having some rather unusual
behaviors. Larvae scurry
about very quickly. They can
switch into reverse and move
just as fast. Adults are a bit
obsessive about cleaning
their legs and antennae. This
behavior is even part of their
courting ritual.

SMALL HEAD   ELONGATED PROTHORAX

CHEWING
MOUTHPARTS

EXPERT'S CIRCLE

DON'T BE FOOLED Female Snakeflies have a long projection sticking out from their
abdomens. It looks like a stinger, but it's not. It's the ovipositor, or the part they use to lay their eggs.

INSECT REPORT
BEETLE MANIA

BEETLES UNDERGO COMPLETE METAMORPHOSIS. ADULTS LAY EGGS IN A VARIETY OF PLACES: IN WOOD, ON LEAVES, UNDER BARK, OR EVEN IN DEAD ANIMAL CARCASSES. THE EGGS HATCH, AND WORMLIKE LARVAE EMERGE. PEOPLE SOMETIMES CALL BEETLE LARVAE "GRUBS." THE LARVAE TURN INTO PUPAE, WHICH EVENTUALLY MATURE INTO ADULTS.

Beetles live everywhere on Earth except for the oceans and Antarctica. They are found in nearly every type of habitat. They are the largest group in the animal kingdom. Nearly one-fourth of all animals on Earth are beetles! Like all insects, beetles have three main body parts: head, thorax, and abdomen. All six legs are attached to the thorax. So are the beetle's wings. Beetles have both front and back wings. Their front wings are thick and hard. They cover and protect most of a beetle's body, while the membranous hind wings are used to fly.

OTHER FAMILIES OF BEETLES CAN SECRETE CHEMICALS THAT CAUSE RASHES AND ITCHING, BUT THE BEETLES ON THIS PAGE DO NOT.

Red Milkweed Beetle

Antennae are important body parts on a beetle. They help the beetle find food, mates, and a safe place to lay eggs. Some beetles, like the Red Milkweed Beetle, have extra-long antennae.

Pennsylvania Firefly

The Pennsylvania Firefly is a beetle. It can do something very few other animals can. It can make its own light. This ability is called bioluminescence.

Rainbow Scarab

Beetles eat just about everything. This Rainbow Scarab eats animal waste.

Dogbane Beetle

Beetles have hard, thick front wings that protect their bodies. Some beetles have other interesting defenses, too. The Dogbane Beetle shoots out a sticky substance that glues potential predators' mouthparts together.

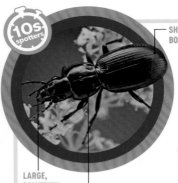

SHINY BLACK BODY AND LEGS

Sidewalk Carabid

Pterostichus melanarius ORDER **Coleoptera** · LENGTH **0.47–0.79 in (12–20 mm)** · HABITAT **Under stones, loose bark, and leaf litter** · RANGE **Atlantic and Pacific coasts** · Complete metamorphosis

LARGE, POWERFUL JAWS

ROUNDED PRONOTUM (PLATE-LIKE STRUCTURE COVERING THE THORAX) WITH SHARP ANGLES AT END

The Sidewalk Carabid, a common black ground beetle, is native to Europe. These beetles originally appeared in urban areas on the East and West Coasts of the United States. But they are quickly spreading to less populated areas in the country. Sidewalk Carabids are predators that eat larvae and insect eggs living in the ground. These beetles prefer to be in open spaces outdoors. You might see them on a sidewalk, as they tend to take the easiest way from one place to another when wandering about. But you might also see them indoors. They can move quickly through an open door.

SIX SMALL WHITE SPOTS ON FOREWINGS

Six-spotted Tiger Beetle

Cicindela sexguttata ORDER **Coleoptera** · LENGTH **0.4–0.6 in (10–15 mm)** · HABITAT **Hardwood forest floor and along woodland paths** · RANGE **Eastern United States and southeastern Canada** · Complete metamorphosis

METALLIC GREEN BODY

The Six-spotted Tiger Beetle has a metallic green body with small white spots on its forewings and shiny green legs. Insects of this species hibernate during winter as adults. They emerge from hibernation when temperatures rise and are most active in the spring. In more populated areas, you might spot one on a sidewalk. In forests, their preferred habitat, they show up along dirt paths and on fallen logs.

Laugh Out Loud!

Why were the Sidewalk Carabids so proud of their new home?

It had great curb appeal.

Emerald Ash Borer

Agrilus planipennis ORDER **Coleoptera**
- LENGTH **0.39–0.51 in (10–13 mm)** ▪ HABITAT **Ash trees**
- RANGE **Northeastern and midwestern United States**
- Complete metamorphosis

In the summer of 2002, Emerald Ash Borers were discovered nibbling on an ash tree in southeastern Michigan. Since then, these pests have spread like wildfire. They are an invasive species that has killed ash trees in half of the states in the United States as well as in several provinces in eastern Canada. The adult beetles are fairly harmless. They nibble on ash leaves. But the larvae feed on the inner bark of ash trees, disrupting the trees' ability to transport water and nutrients.

METALLIC EMERALD GREEN COLOR

HARD FRONT WINGS ARE DARKER, DULLER GREEN.

INSECT inspector!

Emerald Ash Borers are native to Asia. Most likely, they were introduced to the United States on a wooden packing crate that was transported from Asia on a cargo ship or airplane.

BRONZE LUSTER ON UNDERSIDE

Western Sculptured Pine Borer

Chalcophora angulicollis ORDER **Coleoptera** ▪ LENGTH **0.79–1.3 in (20–33 mm)** ▪ HABITAT **Coniferous forests** ▪ RANGE **Western United States**
- Complete metamorphosis

The Western Sculptured Pine Borer has a dark brown to black body with a metallic sheen. Females lay eggs on the bark of weak and dying conifer trees. After eggs hatch, these insects spend up to two years as fat white larvae. The larvae burrow through the wood, leaving tunnels and piles of sawdust below. When adults finally emerge, they buzz through the air and aren't shy about landing on people. Although they don't bite, they do have clingy legs.

DARK BROWN TO BLACK SCULPTURES ON UPPER SIDE

Colorado Potato Beetle

Leptinotarsa decemlineata ORDER Coleoptera ● LENGTH 0.31–0.39 in (8–10 mm) ● HABITAT Farms that grow potatoes, tomatoes, tobacco, eggplants, and peppers ● RANGE East of the Rocky Mountains ● Complete metamorphosis

The Colorado Potato Beetle is a type of leaf beetle. It lives on and eats the leaves of potatoes and related plants. Depending upon how cold it is, it can take anywhere from 14 to 56 days for a Colorado Potato Beetle egg to develop into an adult. Once it becomes an adult, the beetle feeds for a short time and then it mates and reproduces. Because they only live for a few weeks, it's possible to see egg, larva, pupa, and adult stages of these beetles at the same time. Some adults dig into the soil to spend the winter underground. Some females that do this have already mated. Once they emerge in the spring, they can immediately start laying eggs.

INSECT Inspector!

Colorado Potato Beetle larvae bring out all sorts of moves when it comes to deterring predators. They walk away, rear up on their back legs, throw up, wiggle, and even poop to avoid being eaten.

FIVE THICK BROWN STRIPES RUNNING FRONT TO BACK ON EACH HARD, THICK FRONT WING

ORANGE THORAX WITH BLACK SPOTS

10s spotters

SHORT ANTENNAE

Laugh Out Loud!

What do you call a baby Colorado Potato Beetle?

A tater tot.

Dogbane Beetle

Chrysochus auratus ORDER **Coleoptera** • LENGTH **0.27–0.44 in (7–11 mm)** • HABITAT **Open, disturbed areas or along forest edges, lakeshores, and areas with gravelly soil** • RANGE **Eastern United States to the Rocky Mountains, southern Canada** • Complete metamorphosis

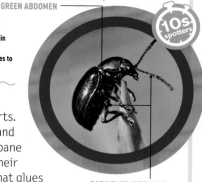

METALLIC GOLDEN GREEN BODY, GREEN ABDOMEN

DARK BLUE ANTENNAE AND LEGS

The metallic golden green Dogbane Beetle has blunt, misaligned mouthparts. This allows it to chew dogbane leaves and drink juice from milkweed plants. Dogbane plants naturally protect themselves. Their leaves hold a sticky, milky substance that glues insects' mouthparts together when it dries. This is no problem for the Dogbane Beetle. Unlike other insects, Dogbane Beetles don't cut leaf veins before they eat. Instead, they eat the outer parts of a leaf. This limits their exposure to the sticky glue. They get some glue on their mouthparts but wipe it off after they eat. They walk backward off the leaf as they do this. This keeps them from getting the sticky glue on their feet. These behaviors help them survive.

Golden Tortoise Beetle

ROUNDED METALLIC GOLD BODY

Charidotella sexpunctata bicolor ORDER **Coleoptera** • LENGTH **0.2–0.28 in (5–7 mm)** • HABITAT **Wherever morning glory plants are found** • RANGE **Throughout the United States and southeastern Canada** • Incomplete metamorphosis

HARD "DOME" OVER BODY

A few amazing adaptations make the Golden Tortoise Beetle hard to forget. First, there's the body. This beetle looks like it has a hard, upside-down bowl on its back. That "bowl" is actually the front wings and part of the thorax. Then there's the behavior. When something disturbs a Golden Tortoise Beetle, it reacts just like a turtle and pulls its legs under the dome. Finally, there's the coloring. The Golden Tortoise Beetle's body is gold—and it can change colors! When something disturbs this beetle, it becomes orange with black spots.

Red Milkweed Beetle

Tetraopes tetrophthalmus ORDER
Coleoptera · LENGTH 0.47–0.59 in (12–15 mm)
· HABITAT Grasslands, gardens, and road edges
where milkweed plants grow · RANGE Throughout
the United States · Complete metamorphosis

The Red Milkweed Beetle
is a type of longhorn beetle.
Beetles in this family have
exceptionally long antennae.
The antennae on a male Red
Milkweed Beetle, for example, are
almost as long as its body. The Red
Milkweed Beetle lives anywhere milkweed plants are found. Adults
eat milkweed leaves, buds, and flowers. The female lays her eggs at
the base of the milkweed stem. Larvae tunnel into the soil and
feed on milkweed roots. They spend the winter underground. Then
they turn into pupae for about a month in the spring. Toxins in the
milkweed plants transfer to the Red Milkweed Beetles as they eat.
Their red and black coloring warns predators to stay away.

→ LISTEN FOR THIS
RED MILKWEED BEETLES rub
parts of their thorax against the
pronotum (a plate-like structure
that covers the thorax) to make
a shrill squeaking sound.

LONG ANTENNAE

RED BODY WITH
BLACK SPOTS

BLACK LEGS

The socket of a Red Milkweed Bug's antenna splits both of its compound eyes in half. The result is an
upper and a lower compound eye on each side. Fittingly, the names of this insect's genus, *Tetraopes,* and
species, *tetrophthalmus,* mean "four eyes" when translated into Latin.

Seven-spotted Lady Beetle

DOMED, OVAL, REDDISH BODY

Coccinella septempunctata ORDER **Coleoptera**
◦ **LENGTH 0.28–0.31 in (7–8 mm)** ◦ **HABITAT Open fields, grasslands, marshes, agricultural fields, and suburban gardens and parks** ◦ **RANGE Throughout the United States** ◦ **Complete metamorphosis**

The Seven-spotted Lady Beetle, which has seven black spots on its red back, is not a native species in the United States. It was intentionally introduced to this country from Europe and Asia in the 1950s because it eats aphids, which can be a major pest to agricultural crops. Twenty years later, the first successful population was discovered in New Jersey. Now, the Seven-spotted Lady Beetle is the most common and widespread lady beetle in the United States. Adults of this species have very few natural enemies.

SEVEN BLACK SPOTS IN
1-4-2 PATTERN ON BACK

Multicolored Asian Lady Beetle

Harmonia axyridis ORDER **Coleoptera** ◦ **LENGTH 0.2–0.31 in (5–8 mm)** ◦ **HABITAT Orchards, forests, row crops, and gardens** ◦ **RANGE Throughout the United States** ◦ **Complete metamorphosis**

The Multicolored Asian Lady Beetle was also introduced to the United States as a natural way to control aphid pests. As a larva, just one of these beetles can eat up to 370 aphids. During its adult lifetime, it may devour up to 5,000 aphids! Recognizing Multicolored Asian Lady Beetles can be difficult. They change both color and pattern during their lifetime. One beetle may be solid orange, orange with black spots, or red with black spots. The number of spots dotting their backs can range from zero to 21!

NO SPOTS UP
TO 21 BLACK SPOTS

ORANGE OR
RED BACK

Unless you're an entomologist, you probably call the insects on this page "ladybugs." That is incorrect. True bugs are insects with sucking mouthparts that undergo incomplete metamorphosis. These insects are beetles. They have chewing mouthparts and undergo complete metamorphosis.

Eyed Click Beetle

Alaus oculatus ORDER **Coleoptera** • LENGTH **0.94–1.8 in (24–45.5 mm)**
• HABITAT **Deciduous woods and areas with many hardwood trees** • RANGE
Eastern United States, west to Texas and South Dakota; Quebec, Canada
• **Complete metamorphosis**

DIFFERENT
COLOR
PATTERNS
ON BACK

The adult Eyed Click Beetle is a true acrobat. This beetle has a hinged joint between its head and thorax. If it accidentally gets flipped over, it arches its back and snaps itself into the air. It can fly up more than four times its own body length! Even without the tumbling moves, this beetle is an interesting sight. It has two eyespots on its pronotum. They're just black spots with white rings, but they look like giant menacing eyes to predators.

→ **LISTEN FOR THIS**
WHAT SOUND DOES an Eyed Click Beetle make? A "click," of course! Click beetles move parts of their thorax against each other. This motion produces a clicking noise that's loud enough to scare off potential predators.

FORKED TEETH

Wireworm

Alaus oculatus ORDER **Coleoptera** • LENGTH **2 in (51 mm)** • HABITAT
The soil in deciduous woods and areas with many hardwood trees
• RANGE **Eastern United States, west to Texas and South Dakota;**
Quebec, Canada • **Complete metamorphosis**

BLACK
HEAD

YELLOWISH
BROWN BODY

Click beetle larvae are called Wireworms. The larvae of the Eyed Click Beetle look like fat segmented worms with six legs. They have smooth, hard-shelled, yellowish brown bodies. Their large black heads are flat and have a pair of forked teeth. Although Wireworms look a bit threatening, there's nothing to worry about unless you're a root or an insect. While many Wireworm species are pests that dine on the roots of cereal crops, larvae of the Eyed Click Beetle like meat. They devour other pest larvae, including young wood-boring beetles and flies.

Japanese Beetle

SHINY METALLIC GREEN BODY

Popillia japonica ORDER **Coleoptera** • LENGTH **0.5 in (12.5 mm)**
• HABITAT **Anywhere with enough foliage to feed on** • RANGE **Eastern United States, except Florida, west to Missouri**
• Complete metamorphosis

In 1916, Japanese Beetles were accidentally introduced to the United States from eastern Asia. Finding a favorable climate, many favorable host plants, and a lack of natural enemies, the species flourished. Now, the Japanese Beetle is a major pest across much of the country. Adults eat the foliage, flowers, and fruits of more than 300 different ornamental and agricultural plants. They lay eggs in the summer and the eggs hatch in late summer and early fall. Growing larvae live underground, where they feast on grass roots.

TUFTS OF WHITE HAIR ON SIDES AND IN BACK OF BODY, UNDER THE EDGES OF THE WINGS

BRONZE-COLORED OUTER WINGS

MALES HAVE HORNS.

Rainbow Scarab

Phanaeus vindex ORDER **Coleoptera** • LENGTH **0.39–0.87 in (10–22 mm)** • HABITAT **Under piles of dung** • RANGE **Eastern United States, west to South Dakota** • Complete metamorphosis

The mouthparts of a Rainbow Scarab are perfectly adapted for eating this insect's favorite food—dung. First, its mouth is big: It's one-third as long as the beetle's head. Also, its jaws have furry, flexible, rounded cutting edges that are perfect tools for munching on soft, mushy poo. To reach dung, adults dig a tunnel and chamber in the soil under a dung pile. They pull soil-coated balls of dung into the chamber to feed larvae and young adults.

BRIGHT GREEN, BLUE, RED, AND GOLDEN METALLIC EXTERIOR

BULKY OVAL BODY

Laugh Out Loud!

What did the Rainbow Scarab say at the end of a long, hard day?

"I sure am pooped!"

Eastern Hercules Beetle

Dynastes tityus ORDER **Coleoptera** ▪ LENGTH **1.57–2.36 in (40–60 mm)** ▪ HABITAT **Hardwood forests** ▪ RANGE **Eastern United States** ▪ **Complete metamorphosis**

MALES: LARGE HEAD HORN AND THREE HORNS ON THORAX

HARD TAN OR GREEN COVERING HAS IRREGULAR PATTERNS OF BLACK SPOTS.

While the Eastern Hercules Beetle may not grow as big as its Central American cousin, the Hercules Beetle, it's still an impressively large insect. Adults can grow up to 2.36 inches (60 mm) long and just over an inch (25.5 mm) wide. Males also have horns. They have one large horn on their head and another large horn surrounded by two smaller horns on their thorax. Larvae can be found on tree stumps or inside hollowed-out trees feeding on decaying wood. Adults have been observed eating rotten fruit and the bark of ash trees.

MALES HAVE LONGER ANTENNAE THAN FEMALES.

Ten-lined June Beetle

Polyphylla decemlineata ORDER **Coleoptera** ▪ LENGTH **0.87–1.18 in (22–30 mm)** ▪ HABITAT **Orchards and areas with sandy soils** ▪ RANGE **Western United States to the Great Plains** ▪ **Complete metamorphosis**

The Ten-lined June Beetle begins life as a large, oval, creamy white egg. It hatches into a C-shaped grub that can grow up to 2 inches (51 mm) long. Grubs munch on roots and grasses. Their feeding frenzies can kill large, mature trees. It takes about two years for grubs to change into pupae and emerge as adults. Adults have brown bodies with long white stripes on their backs. Their bodies are covered with small white hairs. These beetles tend to fly toward lights at night. Although they don't bite, they will hiss loudly if they are disturbed.

BROWN BODY WITH SMALL WHITE HAIRS; LONG WHITE STRIPES ON BACK

Hairy Rove Beetle

Creophilus maxillosus ORDER **Coleoptera**
▪ **LENGTH 0.47–0.63 in (12–16 mm)** ▪ **HABITAT**
Wooded areas and open ground ▪ **RANGE Eastern**
United States ▪ **Complete metamorphosis**

Hairy Rove Beetles have shiny black bodies covered with yellowish gray hairs. They are attracted to the stench of decay and can be found around dung piles, compost heaps, and carrion, which is rotting animal flesh. Yet the beetles don't eat any of these things. They're after the maggots that hatch from the eggs that flies leave behind when they come to feast. As soon as maggots hatch and become active, the beetles appear. To catch their prey, they must move quickly. That's possible because the hard covering over a Hairy Rove Beetle's wings is extremely short. Not only are these beetles fast, but they're also quite flexible.

INSECT inspector!

The Hairy Rove Beetle is one of the insect species that forensic entomologists look for at a crime scene. These beetles hang out around dead bodies and eat maggots. Studying the beetles helps determine what happened and when it occurred.

SHINY BLACK BODY

NEEDLELIKE MANDIBLES

VERY SHORT FRONT WINGS

10s spotters

YELLOWISH GRAY HAIRS (FRONT WINGS AND ABDOMEN)

→ LOOK FOR THIS
ROVE BEETLES are fast fliers. But they can also run quickly over the ground. When they run, they lift the tip of their abdomen into the air, just like a scorpion raises its stinger.

BLACK BODY

10s spotters

END OF ABDOMEN IS WHITE OR YELLOW AND HAS A YELLOWISH GREEN GLOW.

YELLOW EDGING ON THORAX AND FRONT WINGS

Pennsylvania Firefly

Photuris pennsylvanica ORDER **Coleoptera** • LENGTH **0.43–0.59 in (11–15 mm)** • HABITAT **Open forests and meadows** • RANGE **Eastern United States to Texas, north to Manitoba** • **Complete metamorphosis**

During the day, the Pennsylvania Firefly looks pretty much like any other beetle. But at night, it's impossible to miss. These insects are bioluminescent. The end of their abdomen flashes a faint yellowish green light in the summertime darkness. Males flash as they fly through the air, trying to attract a female. Females wait in grass and bushes. If they're interested, they respond. Each species of firefly has its own flash pattern. This one makes a short flash followed by a longer flash seven seconds later.

INSECT inspector!

Female Pennsylvania Fireflies will sometimes imitate and respond to the flash pattern of male Synchronous Fireflies. When the males arrive, the females catch them and eat them.

BLACK MARGIN ON EDGES OF PRONOTUM

10s spotters

AT NIGHT, END OF ABDOMEN HAS YELLOWISH GREEN GLOW.

BLACK, PINK, AND OPAQUE PRONOTUM

Synchronous Firefly

Photinus carolinus ORDER **Coleoptera** • LENGTH **0.31–0.49 in (8–12.5 mm)** • HABITAT **Hardwood forests near streams at higher altitudes** • RANGE **Northern Georgia Appalachian Mountains to western Pennsylvania** • **Complete metamorphosis**

As their name suggests, Synchronous Fireflies are in sync! From about 9:30 p.m. to midnight each night of the two-week mating season, thousands of males light up the sky as a group. They produce four to eight flashes at half-second intervals followed by six to nine seconds of darkness. Females send out a single flash as a response. The females rarely fly but stay hidden in the grass. Males must go to the ground and hope to be selected over their competitors.

Giant Stag Beetle

Lucanus elaphus **ORDER Coleoptera · LENGTH 1.18–2.36 in (30–60 mm) · HABITAT Damp, rotting wood in forests · RANGE Eastern United States, from Maryland to Florida and west to Texas · Complete metamorphosis**

Giant Stag Beetles live in large colonies in rotted-out trees, where females lay their eggs. Larvae eat and grow for several years before turning into pupae. Seven to nine months later, they emerge as adults. The adult form of this beetle is impressive. Both males and females have reddish brown, shiny bodies with wide heads. Males have a crest above their eyes. They also have giant pincerlike jaws with small forked teeth all along the inner edges. These jaws turn into weapons when the males fight one another for access to females. Males rear up on their front legs and spread their jaws wide, ready to take on the opposition.

10s spotters

BLACK ANTENNAE

WIDE HEAD

FLATTENED BACK

REDDISH BROWN, SHINY BODY

BLACK LEGS

MALES HAVE PINCERLIKE MANDIBLES.

INSECT inspector!

Thirty different species of stag beetles live in the United States. Two-thirds of those species live in the western half of the country.

Horned Passalus

Odontotaenius disjunctus ORDER **Coleoptera**
- LENGTH **1.18–1.57 in (30–40 mm)** • HABITAT **Deciduous forests**
- RANGE **Eastern United States and southeastern Canada**
- Complete metamorphosis

The Horned Passalus is a large, glossy black beetle. Its thorax and abdomen are separated in a way that makes it look like the beetle has a narrow waist. These insects can be found year-round living in deeply carved wooden tunnels they have chewed in rotting logs. And they have a family lifestyle that is uncommon among insects. Both males and females take exceptional care of the young. They guard their territory closely, and they move eggs several times, searching for the best place for larvae to hatch. Once larvae hatch, they regurgitate wood for them to eat. To protect vulnerable pupae, they create small holes called cells for each pupa. Then they hide the pupae in their cells by covering them with waste and litter. Young adults stay with their parents until they fully mature.

MAKE THIS!

Use a comb to create your own insect language.

1. Run your fingers across the teeth of a plastic comb. Describe the sound you hear.

2. Pluck the comb in different areas. Then pluck it at some different speeds. Listen carefully to see how the sounds change.

3. Think of five reasons an insect would need to send a message. Write each message down on paper.

4. Find a unique sound for each message on the comb. Record how you created each sound, citing location on the comb, speed, and pattern of movement.

5. Teach your new language to a friend. Then make each sound. Does your friend know what you're saying?

10s. spotters

SHORT, FORWARD-CURVED HOOK ON TOP OF HEAD

SHINY BLACK BODY

GOLDEN HAIRS LINING MIDDLE LEGS, PRONOTUM, AND ANTENNAE

HARD, THICK, DEEPLY GROOVED FRONT WINGS

INSECT inspector!

The Horned Passalus rubs parts of its wing and abdomen together to communicate. By varying the speed and pattern of the movement, it can create up to 17 different sounds. Each sound has a meaning.

Cocklebur Weevil

ANGLED ANTENNAE WITH CLUBS ON THE END

DOWN-CURVING SNOUT

Rhodobaenus quinquepunctatus ORDER **Coleoptera** • **LENGTH 0.20–0.31 in (5–8 mm)** • **HABITAT Agricultural fields or areas with ragweed and cockleburs** • **RANGE Eastern United States and southeastern Canada** • **Complete metamorphosis**

Members of the Curculionidae family, like the Cocklebur Weevil, are plant-eating beetles with long, down-curving snouts. The antennae have small clubs at the end and are bent. This allows the first segment of the antennae to tuck into a special groove on the side of the snout. The Cocklebur Weevil has a red body with black spots. Toward the end of the front wings, the black spots merge into a black patch. The larvae dig their way into the stems and roots of cocklebur and other plants in the sunflower family.

RED BODY WITH BLACK SPOTS AND BLACK PATCH ON WINGTIPS

Black Vine Weevil

BLACK, ELBOWED AND CLUB ANTENNAE

Otiorhynchus sulcatus ORDER **Coleoptera** • **LENGTH 0.35–0.43 in (9–11 mm)** • **HABITAT Greenhouses, nurseries, vineyards, and agricultural crops** • **RANGE Eastern and western United States up to Alaska, through-out Canada** • **Complete metamorphosis**

In the early summer, adult Black Vine Weevils emerge from the soil. Over the next four months, one female can lay up to 800 eggs. She deposits them near the roots of garden and landscape plants, including azaleas and rhododendrons. Adults are flightless and can live for up to three years. They feed on foliage, which can kill buds and cause leaves and flowers to look ragged. But the larvae feast on the roots. This can kill or weaken many plants.

LONG, BROAD SNOUT

HARD, THICK, BLACK FRONTWINGS WITH SMALL PATCHES OF WHITE SCALES

Why do weevils have such great balance?

Because weevils wobble but they don't fall down.

Laugh Out Loud!

INSECT REPORT
BITES & STINGS

Eastern Yellowjacket

In the United States, there are more allergic reactions to yellowjacket stings than to any other insect bite or sting.

It's wise to think twice before inspecting any strange insects. Every living thing needs to defend itself. And for many insects, the best way to do that is to bite or sting potential threats. Most of the time, people's reactions to bites and stings are mild. The spot where you got bitten might turn red, swell, or itch. But sometimes it can be more serious. Bites and stings can cause severe allergic reactions. And some insects carry disease.

Horse Fly

Horse Flies are powerful biters. They're also persistent. A Horse Fly will chase and bite a host until it gets all the blood it needs.

Bed Bug

Bed Bugs bite and suck the blood from human hosts. A person can't feel the bites right away because Bed Bugs inject a numbing substance. Later the bites usually appear in straight lines and are red and itchy.

IT'S NOT UNCOMMON TO GET BITTEN BY A NORTHERN HOUSE MOSQUITO. THESE BITES ITCH. BUT THEY CAN ALSO TRANSFER WEST NILE VIRUS AND OTHER SERIOUS DISEASES. MOST PEOPLE WHO GET WEST NILE VIRUS HAVE MINOR SYMPTOMS, LIKE A FEVER OR HEADACHE. BUT SOME PEOPLE CAN GET REALLY SICK. TO PROTECT YOURSELF FROM MOSQUITO BITES, USE MOSQUITO REPELLENT AND WEAR CLOTHING THAT COVERS YOUR SKIN.

Black-tipped Hangingfly

Hylobittacus apicalis ORDER **Mecoptera**
• LENGTH **0.20–0.31 in (5–8 mm)** • HABITAT **Shaded places along edges of woodlands and in tall grass** • RANGE **New York south to Georgia and west to Oklahoma** • Complete metamorphosis

When a male Black-tipped Hangingfly wants to mate, he has to first search for prey. Females won't show any interest unless the male provides a gift. So the male goes out in search of an insect. Once he catches one—and possibly eats a bit of it himself—he releases pheromones to attract nearby females. If the gift is large enough, she will respond. Because of this curious mating routine, male Black-tipped Hangingflies spend more time flying than females. This increases their risk of getting trapped in spiderwebs. Some males have figured this out. Instead of flying around searching for prey, they imitate the female. When another male approaches, they grab the offered prey and fly away. They can then offer the prey to a female without having to hunt for it themselves.

Hanglingflies have a single large claw at the end of each leg. This makes it impossible for them to stand on their legs. Instead, they use the claws to suspend from leaves or twigs. And that's why these insects are called "hangingflies."

LARGE CLAW AT THE END OF EACH LEG

FIVE EYES: TWO COMPOUND, THREE SIMPLE

FOUR MEMBRANOUS WINGS WITH SEVERAL CROSSVEINS AND BLACK TIPS

PALE YELLOW TO BROWN BODY

10s spotters

Laugh Out Loud! Why did the hangingfly want to go to Hawaii?

He wanted to be a hang-10 fly.

Scorpionfly

Panorpa nebulosa ORDER **Mecoptera** · LENGTH
0.24–0.51 in (6–13 mm) · HABITAT **Shaded woodlands**
with broad-leaved, herbaceous plants · RANGE **Eastern**
United States and Canada · Complete metamorphosis

Scorpionflies are widespread
across the eastern United
States and Canada. Their name
comes from the way a male's
abdomen curls up over his
back—just like a scorpion's.
Scorpionflies are scavengers. They
mainly eat dead or dying insects but
sometimes will venture to eat larger dead
organisms like frogs or mice. Like their
cousin the Black-tipped Hangingfly, male
Scorpionflies must offer a gift of food to a
female before she'll agree to mate. If the
male can't find a dead insect, he'll spit out a
brown liquid and offer it to the female after
it dries. After the pair mates, the female
lays eggs in the soil. Five to 10 days later, the
eggs hatch.

INSECT inspector!

The Scorpionfly's first-stage
larvae have a sharp egg tooth
between their eyes. They use it
to rip the egg open so they can
hatch. After they're born, they
have another unique trait. No
other larva that undergoes
complete metamorphosis has
compound eyes.

LONG
BEAK

CHEWING
MOUTHPARTS

(10s spotters)

END OF A MALE'S ABDOMEN
IS CURVED UPWARD.

ORANGE AND BLACK PATTERNED BODY

→ LOOK FOR THIS
SCORPIONFLIES live in wooded areas with rich soil. The best place to find one is sitting on top of a plant
with large leaves and a soft green stem. These insects prefer the shade and are rarely found in bright, sunny
areas. If you scare a Scorpionfly, it will most likely fly to another leaf. But if the Scorpionfly feels threatened,
it will immediately fall to the ground.

Snow Scorpionfly

Boreus californicus ORDER Mecoptera
• LENGTH 0.12–0.20 in (3–5 mm) • HABITAT High mountain elevations • RANGE Warner Mountains in Modoc County, California • Complete metamorphosis

Snow Scorpionflies are one of the smallest mecopterans. Adults are no more than 0.2 inch (5 mm) long. They are winter insects, appearing on rocky surfaces above 4,000 feet (1,219 m) elevation from December to March. Adults have shiny black bodies which make them easy to spot on the bright white snow. These insects have long beaks and feed on mosses. Because their forewings are short and they have no hind wings, Snow Scorpionflies cannot fly. As with other scorpionflies, males have abdomens that curve over their backs, just like actual scorpions. *Boreus californicus* is the most widely distributed species of all Snow Scorpionflies in western North America.

SHORT WINGS

BLACK BODY

LONG BEAKS

CHEWING MOUTHPARTS

END OF MALE'S ABDOMEN IS CURVED UPWARD.

There are around 30 species of Snow Scorpionflies. They all live in high-altitude forests in the Northern Hemisphere.

Cat Flea

Ctenocephalides felis **ORDER Siphonaptera**
• **LENGTH 0.06–0.08 in (1.5–2 mm)** • **HABITAT In cat and dog fur** • **RANGE Worldwide** • Complete metamorphosis

Cat Fleas have powerful hind legs. And they're tiny. This combination helps these parasites easily run and jump through hair, fur, and feathers as they search for fresh blood. Adults need fresh blood to produce eggs. Once they find a blood source, females can lay a new egg every hour. The dry, smooth eggs fall out of the animal's hair and onto the ground, where they are nearly impossible to find. The larvae are tiny, too, and when they turn into pupae they spin sticky silk cocoons that attract dirt and debris. This camouflage, once again, makes them very hard to see. The easiest way to detect these insects is to watch your pet. If your cat or dog can't stop scratching, it might just have fleas.

INSECT Inspector!

Does your dog have an itch he can't get rid of? If you live in the United States, the main suspect is probably the Cat Flea. Dog Fleas *(Ctenocephalides canis)* do exist, but this flea species lives in Europe. Cat Fleas are found worldwide, and they're happy to attach themselves to any warm-blooded host.

FLAT BODIES

REDDISH BROWN TO BLACK COLOR

WINGLESS

10s. spotters

STRONG HIND LEGS

Laugh Out Loud! How did the flea get to the circus?

He itch-hiked.

House Fly

Musca domestica **ORDER Diptera**
• LENGTH **0.24–.28 in (6–7 mm)** • HABITAT **Near food, garbage, and feces** • RANGE **Worldwide** • Complete metamorphosis

House Flies originated in central Asia. Now they are one of the most widely distributed insects in the world. House Flies live wherever humans do. They lay their eggs on garbage, feces, road kill, and rotting fruits and vegetables. That's what their larvae eat. Adults prefer some of these same foods, but they need them in liquid form. Larvae have chewing mouthparts. An adult's mouthparts are spongelike. If an adult happens to land on a solid food, such as the hot dog you're eating for dinner, it can still eat. It just has to throw up on your food and let its stomach contents break the food down first.

INSECT inspector!

Although many insect species contain the word "fly" in their names, only members of the order Diptera are true flies. These insects have a single pair of wings and sucking or piercing mouthparts. The common names of true flies are written as two words: House Fly, Deer Fly, and Crane Fly. The common names of other species are written as one word: Dragonfly, Scorpionfly, and Mayfly.

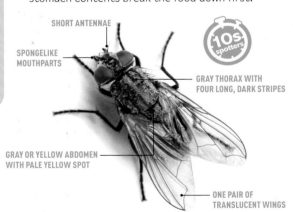

SHORT ANTENNAE

SPONGELIKE MOUTHPARTS

GRAY THORAX WITH FOUR LONG, DARK STRIPES

GRAY OR YELLOW ABDOMEN WITH PALE YELLOW SPOT

ONE PAIR OF TRANSLUCENT WINGS

10s spotters

→ LOOK FOR THIS
HOW CAN YOU tell if a House Fly has regurgitated on your food? Look for light brown spots on your food after the fly leaves. Dark spots mean that the fly has tracked feces to your dinner plate.

Deer Fly

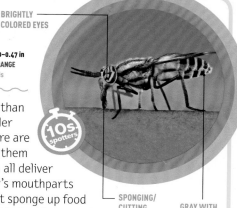

BRIGHTLY COLORED EYES

SPONGING/ CUTTING MOUTHPARTS

GRAY WITH STRIPES LIKE A BEE

Chrysops callidus ORDER Diptera • LENGTH 0.20–0.47 in (5–12 mm) • HABITAT Partly sunny areas near water • RANGE Throughout the United States • Complete metamorphosis

Deer Flies are larger than House Flies but smaller than Horse Flies. There are about 250 different species of them around the world, and they can all deliver a pretty painful bite. A Deer Fly's mouthparts are a combination of parts that sponge up food and parts that work like sharp blades. They use the blades like scissors to cut into skin. Substances in their saliva keep the blood from clotting. This makes it easy for them to lap up the flowing blood. Females are more likely to bite than males. They need the blood to produce viable eggs.

Black Horse Fly

BLACK OR DARK BROWN BODY COVERED WITH SHORT, STOUT HAIRS

Tabanus atratus ORDER Diptera • LENGTH 0.78–0.98 in (20–25 mm) • HABITAT Near aquatic environments • RANGE Throughout the United States • Complete metamorphosis

LARGE COMPOUND EYES (SEPARATED IN FEMALES; CONTINUOUS IN MALES)

PROMINENT MOUTHPARTS WITH SIX DIFFERENT PARTS

When it comes to biting prey, the Black Horse Fly doesn't mess around. Its prominent mouthparts have six different parts. There are two parts for cutting, two parts for piercing, and two parts for sponging up the blood. Like House Flies, female Black Horse Flies need blood to produce viable eggs. So while males feed on nectar, females search for prey. Once the female finds a suitable host, it doesn't stop attacking until it gets all the blood it needs. Black Horse Flies lay eggs near water. One female can lay up to a thousand eggs.

Mediterranean Fruit Fly

Ceratitis capitata • **ORDER Diptera** • **LENGTH 0.12–0.20 in (3–5 mm)** • **HABITAT Agricultural areas that raise fruit** • **RANGE Currently eradicated from the continental United States** • Complete metamorphosis

The Mediterranean Fruit Fly is native to sub-Saharan Africa. It is a highly invasive insect. When it is accidentally brought into the United States—or anywhere else—people react quickly to keep it from spreading. That's because this little fly can cause a whole lot of damage. Females lay their eggs beneath the skin of fruit. Each female lays an average of 300 eggs, and many females tend to lay their eggs in the same place. When the eggs hatch, the larvae carve tunnels as they eat their way through the fruit.

INSECT Inspector!

Mediterranean Fruit Flies are typically introduced to new areas in two ways. They may be present on imported cargo. Or, airline passengers can smuggle infected fruit in their baggage. Once the flies arrive, they're not picky eaters. They've been found on more than 200 different types of fruits and vegetables.

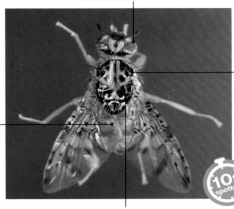

REDDISH PURPLE EYES

CREAMY WHITE THORAX WITH BLACK SPLOTCHES

YELLOWISH BODY WITH BROWN TINGE

BLACK BRISTLES ON OVAL ABDOMEN

10s spotters

Laugh Out Loud!

What does a Mediterranean Fruit Fly call an apple that's falling toward the ground?

Fast food.

Crane Fly

Hexatoma brachycera **ORDER Diptera**
• **LENGTH 0.59–1.1 in (15–28 mm)** • **HABITAT Moist
areas, such as woodlands, streams, and flood plains**
• **RANGE Northeastern United States and eastern
Canada** • Complete metamorphosis

Crane Flies have slender bodies, long legs, and one pair of wings. Their mouthparts look like a long snout. Because of this, people often mistake Crane Flies for giant mosquitoes. They're not. Crane Flies can't bite. Crane Flies are fast-flying flies that swarm near streams and rivers. This is where they lay their eggs. After larvae hatch, they live in the water, where they break down decaying plants. Adults don't eat. Their only focus is to mate. Like all true flies, Crane Flies have a set of antenna-like appendages behind their wings called halteres. Halteres help them keep their balance as they fly through the air.

→ LOOK FOR THIS
CRANE FLIES are attracted to light. So it's not uncommon for them to slip through an open window or door. If they do, you'll probably find them flapping against a lampshade or wall. Just remember: Crane Flies may be big, and they may look like mosquitoes, but they're harmless.

SNOUTLIKE MOUTHPARTS

ELONGATED ANTENNAE

BROWN BODY

LONG, SLENDER, YELLOWISH BROWN LEGS WITH BLACK TIPS

10s spotters

EXPERT'S CIRCLE

DON'T BE FOOLED You don't have to wait to see if you get bitten to tell the difference between a Crane Fly and a mosquito. Mosquitoes have piercing mouthparts and scales on their wing veins. Crane Flies don't. But Crane Flies have a V-shaped groove on the thorax, which mosquitoes lack.

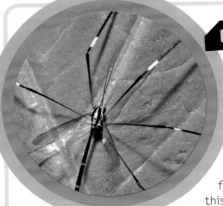

Phantom Crane Fly

Bittacomorpha clavipes **ORDER Diptera**
◦ **LENGTH 0.39–0.55 in (10–14 mm)** ◦ **HABITAT Near swamps
and similar wetlands** ◦ **RANGE East of the Rocky
Mountains** ◦ Complete metamorphosis

With its black and white coloring, the Phantom Crane Fly looks a bit like a mosquito wearing a tuxedo. Its swollen feet could even be the shoes. But this insect isn't a mosquito. It can't bite. And the coloring has a purpose. It helps the Phantom Crane Fly blend in with the mix of shadows and light in its environment. As for the swollen feet, they help this insect fly. When a Phantom Crane Fly takes to the air, it sticks all six legs out perpendicular to the ground. Then it simply flaps its wings as it floats through the air. It can even fly upwind if the breeze isn't too strong.

True **or** False

Q: Phantom Crane Flies are named for the way they float through the air.
A: True. As they float, they seem to appear and disappear. This makes them nearly impossible to detect.

Q: The Phantom Crane Fly's black and white coloring warns potential predators that this insect is poisonous.
A: False. There's nothing toxic here. Those colors just make it easier for this insect to hide.

SWOLLEN "FEET"

BLACK AND WHITE PATTERNED BODY

Phantom Crane Flies spend 20 to 30 days as larvae. During this time, they live in the water. And they breathe through a long tube that they can stick up above the water's surface.

Hover Fly

Toxomerus marginatus **ORDER Diptera**
• **LENGTH 0.19–0.20 in (5–6 mm)** • **HABITAT Near flowering plants** • **RANGE Throughout the United States** • Complete metamorphosis

The Hover Fly is a great example of an insect that uses mimicry for defense. The shape and coloring of this Hover Fly's body make it look like a bee. The easy way tell the difference is to look at the wings. Hover Flies have one set of wings. Bees have two. Plus, this fly doesn't sting. In fact, it's a great insect to have in your garden. The larvae eat aphids and adults feed on pollen and nectar as they pollinate flowers. As these insects fly, they hover in the air, dart forward a short distance, and then hover again. That's why people call them Hover Flies.

→ **LOOK FOR THIS**
SOME HOVER FLIES look like wasps. They even wave their front legs in front of their faces to imitate a wasp's behavior. But like bees, wasps have two sets of wings, while Hover Flies have just one. And wasps sting. Hover Flies don't.

SHORT ANTENNAE

WRAPAROUND COMPOUND EYES

ONE SET OF FOREWINGS WITH STUBBY HALTERES BEHIND

ROUND SPOT NEAR END OF ABDOMEN

BLACK AND YELLOW BODY

10s. spotters

INSECT inspector!

Some people use Hover Flies as a natural way to control insect pests. A large population of Hover Flies can eat between 70 percent and 100 percent of the aphids on a crop.

Bluebottle Fly

Calliphora vomitoria **ORDER Diptera** ◦ **LENGTH 0.4–0.55 in (10 –14 mm)** ◦ **HABITAT Near carrion** ◦ **RANGE Throughout the United States** ◦ Complete metamorphosis

The Bluebottle Fly is a type of blow fly that has an intense attraction to foul-smelling things. It eats dead animals, decaying matter, and poop. It lays its eggs on dead animals or in open wounds because its larvae eat dead meat, too. After the larvae hatch, they feed on the animal for about a week. Adults even pollinate bad-smelling flowers and fungi. In this way, the insect is beneficial. It transfers pollen and spores so these plants and fungi can reproduce. Bluebottle Flies tend to fly in groups. If one fly detects food, it releases a pheromone to let everyone else know that dinner is about to be served.

INSECT Inspector!

Bluebottle Flies are attracted to light, but a pack of these flies isn't likely to swarm inside a house for no reason. Something has to be attracting them. Since these flies love dead and decaying matter, the most likely culprits are a broken sewer line, overflowing garbage, or a dead animal hidden somewhere in the home.

10s spotters

BRIGHT METALLIC BLUE ABDOMEN

CLEAR WINGS

RED EYES

GRAY HEAD AND THORAX

Laugh Out Loud! How do you keep flies out of the kitchen?

Put a pile of garbage in the living room.

Black Fly

Simulium johannseni **ORDER Diptera**
• **LENGTH 0.04–0.2 in (1–5 mm)** • **HABITAT Near rivers and streams** • **RANGE Eastern United States and southeastern Canada** • Complete metamorphosis

Black Flies are tiny insects that have a visible hump behind their heads. Because of that hump, some people call them buffalo gnats. Other people just call them irritating. These little insects tend to swarm around people's heads, and they're not shy about flying into your eyes, ears, or hair. Females feed on blood, so they bite, too. The best way to avoid these swarms is to wear white or brightly colored clothing. Black Flies are attracted to dark colors. Also pay attention to the time of day. They're more likely to swarm at dawn and dusk. If you're lucky, you may be one of the few people who naturally repel Black Flies. These people rarely get bitten.

INSECT inspector!

Black Fly females lay eggs just below the water surface. One female can lay up to 800 eggs. After the eggs hatch, larvae live in the water. Depending on the water temperature, it can take 10 days or several weeks for larvae to develop into pupae. About a week later, pupae emerge as adults. Adults can live up to six weeks.

10s Spotters

STOUT, DARK BODY

HUMP BEHIND THE HEAD

BROAD WINGS

SHORT LEGS

Laugh Out Loud! Why did all the little flies get in trouble?

They were being gnat-ty.

Northern House Mosquito

Culex pipiens **ORDER Diptera** • **LENGTH 0.16–0.39 in (4–10 mm)** • **HABITAT Stagnant water** • **RANGE Northern half of United States, southern Canada** • **Complete metamorphosis**

About 174 species of mosquitoes live in the continental United States. Of those, the Northern House Mosquito is the most common. Like some other insects, males feed on nectar, sap, and honeydew. But females need blood to lay eggs that will grow and survive. They deposit their eggs in pools of stagnant water. Often, the eggs are laid together to create a raft-like structure that floats. It takes two to three days for the eggs to hatch. Then the larvae, which are called wrigglers, live just below the water's surface. They breathe through a tube at the end of their abdomen and filter water through their mouthparts to eat.

True **or** False

Q: Mosquitoes are most active in the winter months.
A: False. Mosquitoes hibernate in winter. They come out in May and bite all summer.

Q: Northern House Mosquitoes are most active in early morning and evening.
A: True

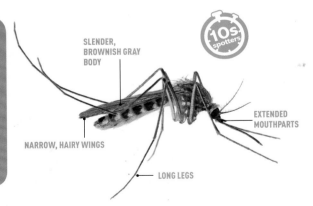

SLENDER, BROWNISH GRAY BODY

EXTENDED MOUTHPARTS

NARROW, HAIRY WINGS

LONG LEGS

10s spotters

INSECT Inspector!

Although the risk is low, you can contract several different illnesses from a Northern House Mosquito bite. In humans, these illnesses include West Nile virus, St. Louis encephalitis, and western equine encephalitis. These mosquitoes can also pass along larvae that cause heartworm in dogs.

Speckled Peter

Helicopsyche borealis ORDER **Trichoptera**
• LENGTH **0.20–0.28 in (5–7 mm)** • HABITAT **In and near fast-flowing rivers and streams, shallow lakes, thermal springs** • RANGE **Throughout the United States and southern Canada, north to the Northwest Territories**
• Complete metamorphosis

The Speckled Peter is a snail-case caddisfly. That means its larvae create cases out of sand and gravel to protect them as they develop. The larvae spiral up inside their cases, making them look like snail shells (right). These larvae are extremely tolerant to temperature changes. They can survive in cold waters and in hot springs up to 110°F (43°C). As adults, these caddisflies are easy to recognize. When the adult Speckled Peter flies, it looks different from every other caddisfly. Its four wings move together instead of as two separate sets. That's because this caddisfly's top wings are attached to its bottom wings by a row of hooks.

INSECT inspector!

Caddisfly larvae protect themselves in different ways. Some build cases around their bodies that may look like snail shells, long tubes, or log cabins. Others spin cases of silk. Some are predators who don't need cases—they stay free to hunt.

CHEWING MOUTHPARTS

PAIR OF HOOKED LEGS AT TIP OF ABDOMEN

CATERPILLAR-LIKE BODY

10s spotters

PROTECTED BY SAND AND GRAVEL CASE

→ **LOOK FOR THIS**
CADDISFLY LARVAE look so similar—both as larvae and adults—that it's hard to tell them apart. Sometimes it's much easier to identify a caddisfly species by looking at the case the larvae built.

INSECT REPORT
THE ART OF DECEPTION

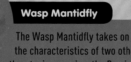

Wasp Mantidfly

The Wasp Mantidfly takes on the characteristics of two other threatening species, the Praying Mantis and the paper wasp. If a predator approaches, it will even act like a wasp ready to attack.

All living things need to protect themselves. Insects are no exception. Some insects do bite and sting potential predators. But others have mastered the art of deception. They rely on mimicry, camouflage, and deceptive behaviors to keep them safe from harm.

Shore Earwig

When the Shore Earwig is threatened, it spits out an odor that smells like rotting flesh!

THE GIANT WALKINGSTICK BLENDS IN WITH ITS ENVIRONMENT. IT LOOKS JUST LIKE A PART OF A BRANCH.

Luna Moth

The Luna Moth is large. But the giant eyespots on its back make it look bigger and scarier to potential predators.

Tulip-tree Beauty

The colors of a Tulip-tree Beauty blend in perfectly with a tree. This moth also holds its wings flat, making it nearly impossible to see.

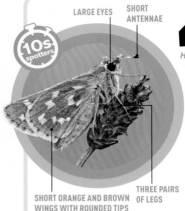

LARGE EYES **SHORT ANTENNAE**

Common Branded Skipper

Hesperia comma ORDER **Lepidoptera** • LENGTH **1.13–1.25 in (28.5–32 mm)**
• HABITAT **Sunny fields, meadows, and forest openings** • RANGE **Central Alaska east to Labrador, south to the northern Rocky Mountains, Great Lakes states, and Maine** • Complete metamorphosis

SHORT ORANGE AND BROWN WINGS WITH ROUNDED TIPS **THREE PAIRS OF LEGS**

The Common Branded Skipper is a medium-size butterfly that loves sunny places. It flies rapidly through the air, fluttering its wings so quickly that they appear to blur. Adults have short orange and brown wings with rounded tips. The underside of the wings shimmers and has white spots. Like many other butterflies, males perch on tall plants or hilltops and wait for interested females to approach. Females lay their eggs on or near a host plant. Adults drink the nectar of asters, goldenrods, and other flowers. Caterpillars eat grasses and leaves.

SHORT ANTENNAE
LARGE EYES

Mottled Duskywing

Erynnis martialis ORDER **Lepidoptera** • LENGTH **1.13–1.63 in (28.5–41.5 mm)** • HABITAT **Open woodlands, hills, and fields** • RANGE **Eastern United States, southern Canada** • Complete metamorphosis

SCENT SCALES ON ABDOMEN **DARK BROWN WINGS WITH IRREGULAR PATCHES OF BLACK AND A PURPLE SHINE**

Mottled Duskywings are skipper butterflies. They have dark brown wings with irregular patches of black and a purple shine. Both males and females have scent scales on their bodies. To find mates, males fly to the highest point on a hill or ridge and then wait for females to fly by. As the males wait, they hold their wings straight out. Females lay two batches of eggs in summer. Offspring in the first batch are smaller than those born later.

Laugh Out Loud!

What do you call a butterfly that you saw yesterday?

A butter-flew.

Western Pygmy-Blue

Brephidium exilis ORDER **Lepidoptera** • LENGTH **0.5–0.75 in (12.5–19 mm)** • HABITAT **Deserts, salt marshes, wastelands, and other alkaline areas** • RANGE **Western United States**
• Complete metamorphosis

WINGS COPPERY BROWN ON TOP, SPOTTED BLACK BENEATH

DULL BLUE COLORING AT BASE OF WINGS ON BODY'S TOPSIDE

Depending upon which source you use, the Western Pygmy-Blue could be identified as the smallest butterfly in the world. After all, its wingspan doesn't get bigger than three-quarters of an inch (19 mm). This butterfly has coppery brown wings. On the topside, the wings are dull blue at the base. Underneath, they have white fringe and black spots. Caterpillars of this species can secrete a sugary substance that attracts ants. If a predator approaches, the caterpillars release a chemical that smells just like the chemical ants use to warn each other about incoming danger. This excites the ants so they attack, protecting the caterpillar from harm.

TWO-TONE BROWN WINGS

STRIPED ANTENNAE

SIX LEGS

STUBBY TAIL ON HIND WINGS

Henry's Elfin

Callophrys henrici ORDER **Lepidoptera** • LENGTH **1–1.25 in (25.5–32 mm)** • HABITAT **Edges and openings in barrens and near pine or pine-oak forests** • RANGE **Eastern North America** • Complete metamorphosis

Although widespread, the Henry's Elfin butterfly can be difficult to find. Two of the best places to look are on red bud and willow trees. Females commonly lay their eggs here so caterpillars can eat the buds and young leaves. As for the adults, they like to drink the nectar that the flowers on these trees produce. Henry's Elfin butterflies have brown wings. The inner wings are two-toned in shades resembling chocolate and cinnamon. The outer wings are a rich toasty brown. Caterpillars are light green but change to a dark reddish brown color shortly before becoming pupae.

Monarch

Danaus plexippus ORDER **Lepidoptera** • LENGTH **3.38–4.86 in (86–123.5 mm)** • HABITAT **Open areas with flowers and host plants** • RANGE **East and west of the Rocky Mountains** • Complete metamorphosis

UPPER SIDE OF WINGS IS BRIGHT ORANGE WITH BLACK VEINS.

BLACK WING BORDERS HAVE WHITE SPOTS.

Few insects are as widely recognized as the orange and black Monarch butterfly. Eastern adult Monarchs fly thousands of miles to spend the winter in Mexico, where they breed. Along the way, groups stop to rest and feed together. Females lay eggs on milkweed plants. Monarchs absorb poison from the milkweed plant, but it doesn't bother them. But it does make them taste bad to potential predators.

→ **SAVE THE MONARCHS**
THE MONARCH BUTTERFLY population has dropped from 1 billion to less than 60 million butterflies, mainly because of loss of habitat. To help, people are creating habitats by planting milkweed along Monarch migration paths.

SINGLE ROW OF WHITE DOTS

Viceroy

Limenitis archippus ORDER **Lepidoptera** • LENGTH **2.5–3.38 in (63.5– 86 mm)** • HABITAT **Open or slightly shrubby areas near water** • RANGE **Eastern United States into the Cascade Mountains, central Canada, northern Mexico** • Complete metamorphosis

BLACK LINE ACROSS THE HIND WING

ORANGE WINGS WITH BLACK BORDERS AND VEINS

The Viceroy butterfly is a master of mimicry. Where it coexists with Monarchs, it looks just like a small Monarch butterfly. In other parts of its range, it takes on the appearance of Queen *(Danaus gilippus)* or Soldier *(Danaus eresimus)* butterflies. People once believed that imitating a poisonous butterfly like the Monarch would protect the Viceroy from predators. But studies show that the Viceroy actually tastes worse to predators than any of the other butterflies that it imitates. So they might benefit from the Viceroy's mimicry!

Question Mark

Polygonia interrogationis · **ORDER Lepidoptera** · **LENGTH 2.2–3 in (56–76 mm)**
· **HABITAT Wooded areas with open space**
· **RANGE Eastern United States and southern Canada** · Complete metamorphosis

The Question Mark butterfly has a very appropriate name. On the underside of its wings, it has a white spot shaped like a question mark. With its wings open, this butterfly has a beautiful reddish orange body with black spots. But when the wings are closed, the Question Mark butterfly looks a lot like a leaf. It's even shaped like a decaying leaf. These butterflies live in wooded areas with open space. You might see one in a city park. Unlike many butterflies, Question Marks aren't naturally attracted to flowers. They prefer to sip liquids from rotting fruit, tree sap, dung, and rotting animal flesh.

UPPER SIDE OF WINGS IS REDDISH ORANGE WITH BLACK SPOTS.

UNDERSIDE OF WINGS IS LIGHT BROWN AND HAS A WHITE QUESTION MARK IN THE CENTER.

TAIL ON HIND WING

→ LOOK FOR THIS THE QUESTION MARK belongs to the Nymphalidae family of butterflies. The front legs of these butterflies are too short to be used for walking. Wings can have irregular shapes or even tail-like projections. Brown, orange, yellow, and black are the most common colors. Some adults live up to 11 months, making these some of the longest-living butterflies.

Laugh Out Loud!

Why did the Question Mark butterfly fail the history test?

He didn't have any answers.

Black Swallowtail

ROWS OF YELLOW, BLUE, AND RED SPOTS AND BARS

BLACK WINGS

THREE PAIRS OF WALKING LEGS

TAILS ON WINGS

Papilio polyxenes ORDER **Lepidoptera** • LENGTH **3.25–4.25 in (82.5–108 mm)** • HABITAT **Open areas such as fields, marshes, deserts, and roadsides** • RANGE **Most of North America** • Complete metamorphosis

Black Swallowtails are usually seen between April and October. Every day, the male chooses a new territory. It perches high on a hilltop and patrols the flat areas below to find a mate. As a female approaches, the two butterflies flutter around each other. Then the mating begins. Later, the female lays round, cream-colored eggs on plants such as Queen Anne's lace, carrots, and dill. Larvae eat the leaves of these plants and then hibernate as a chrysalis. The adults that eventually emerge have black wings with yellow, red, and blue spots.

Western Tiger Swallowtail

YELLOW WINGS WITH THICK BLACK BANDS

Papilio rutulus ORDER **Lepidoptera** • LENGTH **2.75–4 in (70–101.5 mm)** • HABITAT **Urban gardens and parks, rural woodlands, and near rivers and streams** • RANGE **Western United States and southwestern Canada** • Complete metamorphosis

TWO BLUE AND ORANGE SPOTS AT THE WING TIPS

TAILS ON WINGS

The Western Tiger Swallowtail drinks nectar from flowers, including thistles, California buckeyes, zinnias, and abelias. It is a very active butterfly that glides from host to host, rarely stopping to rest. Females lay shiny green eggs that are shaped like spheres. Caterpillars have bright green bodies. They have yellow dots and two big yellow eyespots with blue centers on their heads. And there's a black and yellow band with rows of little blue spots around their necks. Caterpillars turn brown just before hibernating in a chrysalis. Western Tiger Swallowtails keep the more vibrant coloring as adults.

Large Tolype Moth

Tolype velleda ORDER Lepidoptera • LENGTH 1.26–2.38 in (32–60.5 mm) • HABITAT Around broadleaf trees and shrubs • RANGE Eastern United States and southeastern Canada • Complete metamorphosis

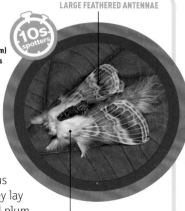

LARGE FEATHERED ANTENNAE

HEAD AND FRONT AND SIDES OF THORAX COVERED IN WHITE HAIR

"Hairy" is the perfect word for the Large Tolype Moth. The head, body, and legs are covered with thick white hair! And the middle of the thorax contains wiry black scales. These moths aren't big, but they're memorable. Large Tolype Moths take flight in September and October. They lay their eggs around ash, birch, elm, oak, and plum trees. Larvae feed on the leaves. Adults stay around these trees to find a mate and reproduce.

CHEWING MOUTHPARTS

Eastern Tent Caterpillar

Malacosoma americanum ORDER Lepidoptera • LENGTH 1.57–1.97 in (40–50 mm) • HABITAT In forests and in trees around homes • RANGE East of the Rocky Mountains • Complete metamorphosis

LONG HAIRS (LOOK FUZZY)

BLACK WITH WHITE STRIPE ON BACK; MAY HAVE BLUE SPOTS ON SIDES

As adults, the Eastern Tent Caterpillars don't get noticed very much. It's the caterpillar stage where these insects take center stage. As spring arrives, females lay masses of eggs on small branches or twigs. After the caterpillars hatch, they move to shrubs or the forks of small branches and spin large silk tents. They stay there for up to six weeks, feeding on newly emergent leaves. Then they leave the tent and spin cocoons. It takes about a month for a pupa to turn into an adult. Adults live for about five days.

Laugh Out Loud! What was the Eastern Tent Caterpillar's favorite subject in school?

Moth-amatics!

LARGE FEATHERED ANTENNAE

LARGE YELLOWISH
GREEN TO PALE BLUISH
GREEN WINGS

LONG, CURVING
TAIL ON EACH
HIND WING

Luna Moth

Actias luna ORDER **Lepidoptera** · LENGTH **2.95–4.13 in (75–105 mm)**
· HABITAT **Deciduous hardwood forests** · RANGE **Eastern United States and southeastern Canada** · Complete metamorphosis

Many people consider the Luna Moth to be the most beautiful moth in North America. The colors in its large wings range from yellowish green to pale bluish green. Each wing has a transparent eye-spot. And the hind wings have long curving tails. To top it all off, their antennae are long and feathery. Luna Moths are nocturnal and aren't easy to find during the daytime. The best place to look is in and around a forest. They are attracted to lights at night. They particularly like hickory, walnut, sumac, and persimmon trees.

REDDISH ORANGE HIND
WINGS WITH YELLOW SPOT

Regal Moth

Citheronia regalis ORDER **Lepidoptera** · LENGTH **3.93–6.3 in (100–160 mm)**
· HABITAT **Deciduous hardwood forests** · RANGE **Eastern United States**
· Complete metamorphosis

It's hard to believe that an insect called the Regal Moth could emerge from a caterpillar called a Hickory Horned Devil. It's even harder to believe when you compare the two. Regal Moths have olive-gray forewings with red veins. Their reddish orange hind wings are speckled with yellow spots. But the larvae look ferocious! Their bluish green bodies contain rows of short black spikes. They have two longer orange spines just behind their heads. And these larvae can stretch up to 5.5 inches (14 cm) long! Hickory Horned Devils feed all summer long. Luckily, they like to eat alone, which limits the amount of damage to host plants. And despite their looks, they're harmless to humans.

OLIVE-GRAY
FOREWINGS
WITH RED VEINS

Isabella Tiger Moth

Pyrrharctia isabella ORDER **Lepidoptera** • LENGTH **1.77–2.56 in (45–65 mm)** • HABITAT **Open parkland and prairies** • RANGE **Widespread across the United States and southern Canada** • Complete metamorphosis

The caterpillars of the Isabella Tiger Moth are famous in North America. They're about 2 inches (51 mm) long and fuzzy, with black and orange bands. You might know them as the Banded Woolly Bear! Some people believe that the thickness of the orange band predicts how severe the coming winter will be. It's a sign of the caterpillar's age. The orange band gets wider each time the caterpillar molts. Caterpillars pupate in the spring. Adults have yellowish brown wings with spots.

ADULT MOTHS HAVE YELLOWISH BROWN WINGS.

TRANSPARENT WINGS PATTERNED WITH BLACK

Scarlet-bodied Wasp Moth

Cosmosoma myrodora ORDER **Lepidoptera** • LENGTH **1.18–1.38 in (30–35 mm)** • HABITAT **Coastal plains** • RANGE **Florida and along the Gulf Coast** • Complete metamorphosis

Male Scarlet-bodied Wasp Moths give females a strange present when they mate: poison. At mating time, the adult male moth visits a dog fennel plant. Scarlet-bodied Wasp Moths are immune to the poison in this plant. As the male feeds, he stores toxins from the plant in small pouches on his underbelly. Then he flies above a female and releases the toxins like a mist. The poisonous mist protects the moths from predators as they mate. During mating, the male transfers poison to the female. She then passes the poison along to her eggs.

SCARLET RED THORAX AND ABDOMEN

Common Gray

Anavitrinella pampinaria ORDER **Lepidoptera** • LENGTH **0.91–0.94 in (23–24 mm)** • HABITAT **Clover and apple, ash, elm, pear, poplar, and willow trees** • RANGE **Throughout North America except the Arctic** • Complete metamorphosis

As adults, Common Gray moths have whitish gray wings with irregular patches of darker brown colors. This makes these moths difficult to spot as they rest on trees. As caterpillars, they look like twigs. The easiest way to spot them is to wait until they move. Caterpillars in the Geometridae family

MEDIUM GRAY TO LIGHT YELLOWISH GRAY WINGS WITH DARK MOTTLING

WHITE BAND ON FIRST ABDOMINAL SEGMENT

are called inch worms. That's because of how they move. These caterpillars only have two back legs. To move, they extend the front part of their bodies as far forward as they can. Then they scrunch the back up from behind. They literally inch their way along.

Tulip-tree Beauty

Epimecis hortaria ORDER **Lepidoptera** • LENGTH **1.7–2.17 in (43–55 mm)** • HABITAT **Pawpaw, poplar, sassafras, and tulip trees** • RANGE **Eastern United States and southeastern Canada** • Complete metamorphosis

You might expect a moth named the Tulip-tree Beauty to have bright floral colors. This moth is brown and ivory. But that doesn't mean it's not beautiful in its own way. The colors of the Tulip-tree Beauty are arranged in zig-zag patterns all over its scalloped wings. These

SCALLOPED MARGIN ON HIND WING

BROWN AND IVORY COLORS IN ZIGZAG PATTERNS

colors and patterns work together to mimic bark on a tree. Tulip-tree Beauties lay their wings completely flat when they rest. This makes them nearly impossible to see, even when they're not settled on a tulip tree.

Laugh Out Loud! Where did the Common Gray moth dream of going someday?

To the moth ball.

White-lined Sphinx

Hyles lineata ORDER **Lepidoptera** · LENGTH **2.44–3.56 in (62–90.5 mm)** · HABITAT **Deserts, meadows, and gardens** · RANGE **Throughout the United States and southern Canada** · Complete metamorphosis

The White-lined Sphinx is a strong, fast flier. From dusk to dawn, it hovers over flowers as it feeds. It can be spotted near flowers with longer petals, including the four o'clock and evening primrose. The moth's long proboscis allows it to drink the nectar deep inside. This relatively large moth is quite attractive. The forewings are dark olive-brown and lined with tan bands. They have white streaks along the veins. The hind wings are black and have a reddish pink band running down the middle.

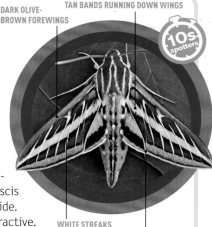

DARK OLIVE-BROWN FOREWINGS

TAN BANDS RUNNING DOWN WINGS

WHITE STREAKS ALONG VEINS

HIND WINGS ARE BLACK WITH PINK BAND DOWN THE MIDDLE.

10s. spotters

BLURRY BROWN AND GRAY FOREWINGS

Five-spotted Hawk Moth

Manduca quinquemaculata ORDER **Lepidoptera** · LENGTH **3.54–5.31 in (90–135 mm)** · HABITAT **Tobacco fields, vegetable gardens, and wherever host plants are found** · RANGE **Throughout the United States and southern Canada** · Complete metamorphosis

The Five-spotted Hawk Moth is a big brown and gray moth. Its forewings look blurry and its hind wings are covered with sharp zigzag lines. When it opens its wings, the reason for its name becomes apparent. The abdomen contains five pairs of bright yellow spots. The larvae of these moths are called Tomato Hornworms. Their fat green bodies have eight V-shaped stripes on them. And there's a big black horn sticking up from the end of the abdomen. These caterpillars have a healthy appetite and can become pests.

10s. spotters

FIVE PAIRS OF YELLOW SPOTS ON ABDOMEN

HIND WINGS HAVE BANDS OF BROWN AND TWO ZIGZAG LINES.

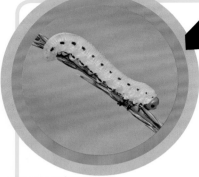

Redheaded Pine Sawfly

Neodiprion lecontei **ORDER Hymenoptera**
• **LENGTH** 0.2–0.33 in (5–8.5 mm) • **HABITAT Pine, cedar, and fir trees** • **RANGE Eastern United States, southern Canada**
• **Complete metamorphosis**

The Redheaded Pine Sawfly is related to wasps and bees. But it doesn't sting. Instead, the female's ovipositor is serrated like a saw. She uses that "saw" to make slits in pine needles where she lays her eggs. One female can lay up to 120 eggs at a time. Each egg is deposited inside its own slit. It takes about two to three weeks for the larvae to hatch. At first they have white bodies with brown heads. As they mature, their bodies become yellowish green with six rows of black spots. Their heads turn red. Larvae feast on the pine tree's needles.

REDDISH-BROWN HEAD

BROAD, BLACK ABDOMEN

10s spotters

MAKE THIS!

Metamorphosis Plate

Round up: 1 paper plate, crayons or markers

1. Trace the flat bottom on the front and the back of the paper plate. You should now have two circles.

2. Draw three lines to divide the circle on the front into thirds. Draw four lines to divide the circle on the back into fourths.

3. Write "Incomplete Metamorphosis" on the outer rim of the front circle. Write "Complete Metamorphosis" on the outer rim of the back circle.

4. Then label the sections. For incomplete metamorphosis, write "egg," "nymph," and "adult." For complete metamorphosis, write "egg," "larva," "pupa," and "adult."

5. Draw arrows between the sections on each side of the plate to show that metamorphosis is a process.

6. Pick one insect that undergoes incomplete metamorphosis and another that undergoes complete metamorphosis.

7. Conduct research to learn how these insects change as they develop.

8. Draw pictures on the correct side of the paper plate to show what each insect looks like during each stage of its life cycle.

9. Write the insect's name on the outer rim of the paper plate.

INSECT Inspector!

Redheaded Pine Sawfly larvae feed on hard pine trees, but they will eat other types of conifers, too. These larvae are attracted to trees growing in large groups. They prefer young trees and can cause a lot of damage to businesses that grow many rows of the same kind of tree. By the time these larvae are finished feasting, once healthy trees can look like towers of dried straw.

Eastern Yellowjacket

Vespula maculifrons ORDER **Hymenoptera** • LENGTH **0.49–0.71 in (12.5–18 mm)** • HABITAT **Forests, meadows, urban and suburban environments** • RANGE **East of the Great Plains** • **Complete metamorphosis**

YELLOW AND BLACK STRIPES ON ABDOMEN

STINGER AT END OF ABDOMEN

CHEWING AND SUCKING MOUTHPARTS

Eastern Yellowjackets are subterranean wasps. Although they do build nests in walls or tree stumps, most colonies are underground. In spring, a queen starts a new colony by building a nest and laying eggs. The first-generation eggs develop into female workers who help expand the nest. Later, the queen lays eggs that develop into males and females—some 5,000.

CHEWING AND SUCKING MOUTHPARTS

European Hornet

Vespa crabro ORDER **Hymenoptera** • LENGTH **0.98–1.38 in (25–35 mm)** • HABITAT **Hollow trees and sheltered cavities** • RANGE **Eastern United States to North and South Dakota** • **Complete metamorphosis**

LARGE, ROBUST BODY WITH REDDISH BROWN PATTERNS

STINGER AT END OF BLACK AND ORANGE STRIPED ABDOMEN

The European Hornet was first introduced to the United States in 1840. It is the only true hornet species found in the United States. Each spring, fertilized queens start a new colony. Nests are typically built in hollow trees or open areas between walls. The nest entrance is usually 6 feet (1.8 m) or more above the ground. Workers of this species drink sap or nectar, which are high-energy foods. They fly around at night capturing insects to feed developing larvae. Once a queen has enough workers in place, she focuses solely on laying eggs.

DANGER!

Eastern Yellowjackets are aggressive stingers. These wasps will attack in swarms if they feel threatened. In the United States, yellowjackets cause more allergic reactions than any other insect. There are three to four times more deaths from reactions to their stings than there are from poisonous snakebites.

Northern Paper Wasp

Polistes fuscatus ORDER **Hymenoptera** ▪ LENGTH **0.59–0.83 in (15–21 mm)** ▪ HABITAT **Woodlands, savannas, in and around homes** ▪ RANGE **Northern United States, southern Canada** ▪ **Complete metamorphosis**

Building a nest is a joint venture for the Northern Paper Wasp. One fertile female begins out of bits of wood, and other fertile females join her. But the original female holds all the power. She becomes the queen. Once the nest is finished, she will either drive the other fertile females away or keep them around as workers. They take care of the queen and her offspring. The queen uses threatening poses to keep her underlings in line. Although the other fertile females can lay eggs, their eggs don't survive. These wasps produce a chemical when they lay eggs. That chemical makes it easy for the queen to figure out which eggs are hers. So when another fertile female lays eggs, the queen eats them.

10s spotters

STINGER AT END OF ABDOMEN

DARK REDDISH BROWN BODY WITH YELLOW BANDS

POINTED HEAD WITH YELLOW MARKING; CURVED ANTENNAE

SLENDER BODY WITH A WAIST BETWEEN THE THORAX AND ABDOMEN

Laugh Out Loud!

Why was the wasp wearing a Band-Aid?

If got a buzz cut.

Black and Yellow Mud Dauber

Sceliphron caementarium ORDER **Hymenoptera** ▪ LENGTH **0.94–1.1 in (24–28 mm)** ▪ HABITAT **Near flowers, around sheltered locations, at pools or puddle edges** ▪ RANGE **Throughout North America** ▪ Complete metamorphosis

The Black and Yellow Mud Dauber is sometimes called the Thread-waisted Wasp. It's easy to see why. This wasp has a very long and narrow waist. Mud daubers are solitary wasps. Each female builds her own home. To do this, she flies back and forth to puddles to collect small balls of mud. She packs the mud together to create a nest of long, narrow cells. Then she lays one egg in each cell. To keep the eggs safe, she plugs the end of each cell with mud. Once the eggs hatch, she flies out in search of spiders. When she spots one, she paralyzes it with a sting. Then she carries the spider home to feed her growing larvae.

INSECT inspector!

Black and Yellow Mud Daubers are not aggressive wasps. But they will sting if you hold them or they become trapped against your body. Fortunately, their sting isn't as painful as the sting of other wasps and bees.

10s spotters

EXTREMELY LONG AND NARROW WAIST

STINGER AT END OF ABDOMEN

GOLDEN BROWN WINGS

LONG BLACK ANTENNAE

BLACK BODY   YELLOW LEGS

→ **LOOK FOR THIS**
BLACK AND YELLOW MUD DAUBERS build their nests in dry, sheltered locations. You can often find them in the corners of buildings or under the eaves. They also build nests on rock ledges and cliff faces and in the hollows of trees.

BLACK ANTENNAE   REDDISH ORANGE ABDOMEN

BLACK HEAD AND THORAX   EXTREMELY LONG BLACK OVIPOSITOR IN FEMALES

10s spotters

Ichneumon Wasp

Dolichomitus irritator ORDER **Hymenoptera** • LENGTH **0.87 in (22 mm)** • HABITAT **Woodlands and brush** • RANGE **Eastern North America** • **Complete metamorphosis**

The species *Dolichomitus irritator* is an intimidating looking wasp. The wasp itself is just under an inch (25.5 mm) long. But the female has a long, black, needlelike projection at the end of her abdomen that looks like a big, scary stinger. It's not. While these wasps do have stingers, that needle is the female's ovipositor. *Dolichomitus irritator* is a parasitic wasp. Females use their extra-long ovipositors to deposit eggs in hosts, including longhorn beetles, weevils, and some wasp look-alikes. After the eggs hatch, the larvae feed on the host.

....

FEMALE HAS LONG OVIPOSITOR.   TRANSPARENT WINGS

10s spotters

Giant Ichneumon Wasp

Megarhyssa macrurus ORDER **Hymenoptera** • LENGTH **2 in (51 mm)** • HABITAT **Deciduous forests** • RANGE **Northeastern and central United States, southeastern Canada** • **Complete metamorphosis**

The Giant Ichneumon Wasp's body is about 2 inches (51 mm) long. The female's ovipositor is twice that long! And her behavior as she tries to lay her eggs has earned this species the nickname "Stump Stabber." These are parasitic wasps, and the female is after the larvae of a wood-boring beetle. First, she searches wood to find a place where the beetle has drilled a hole. Next, she inspects the drilling location with her antennae. Then she gets into position, lifts her abdomen, and inserts her ovipositor vertically into the hole. If she gets stuck, she tries again.

REDDISH BROWN BODY WITH BLACK AND YELLOWISH ORANGE STRIPES

Braconid Wasp

Dinocampus coccinellae ORDER
Hymenoptera • **LENGTH 0.12 in (3 mm)** • **HABITAT**
Wherever lady beetles are found • **RANGE**
Worldwide • **Complete metamorphosis**

Dinocampus coccinellae may be a tiny parasitic wasp, but it's big enough to turn a lady beetle into a zombie! When it reproduces, the female wasp lands on a lady beetle and inserts her ovipositor into the beetle's abdomen. She lays just one egg. After the egg hatches, the larva starts eating the beetle's insides. When it's ready, the wasp larva breaks through the beetle's abdomen. It's not done with the beetle, though. It spins a cocoon between the beetle's legs (right). This partially paralyzes the beetle and gives it no choice but to guard the cocoon until the adult wasp emerges and flies off to find a new host.

It's rare for a parasite to have both physical and behavioral control over a host. It's even more uncommon for a host to stay alive through this experience. Some lady beetles that have been controlled by the *Dinocampus coccinellae* do recover from their ordeal.

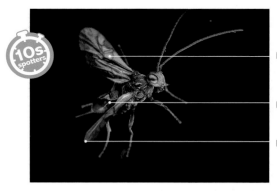

DARK, TRANSPARENT WINGS

BLACK BODY

LONG OVIPOSITOR

→ **LOOK FOR THIS**
ADULT *DINOCAMPUS COCCINELLAE* are rarely seen. The best way to find out if this parasitic wasp is around is to examine a nonmoving lady beetle. There might be a wasp cocoon growing underneath.

Red Velvet Ant

Dasymutilla occidentalis ORDER **Hymenoptera**
• LENGTH **0.79–0.98 in (20–25 mm)** • HABITAT **Fields,
meadows, sandy areas, and long forest edges** • RANGE
Florida to Connecticut, west to Missouri and Texas
• **Complete metamorphosis**

The Red Velvet Ant looks like a hairy red ant with black stripes. It crawls around on the ground like an ant. It even has the word "ant" in its name. But it's not an ant. It's a parasitic wasp that preys on other insects. Female Red Velvet Ants don't have wings. But they do have a powerful stinger. As they crawl around, they search for bumble bee nests. When they find one, they dig into the nesting chamber, chew through the cocoon, and lay their eggs. When the wasp's larvae hatch, they eat the bumble bee larvae and pupae. The wasps don't emerge from the bumble bee nests until they become adults.

DANGER!

The bright red colors on this insect are a warning: Do not touch! While the winged males are harmless, the wingless females aren't. They have a long stinger. If you touch a female or step on one with your bare feet, it will really hurt.

BRIGHT RED, FURRY HEAD, THORAX, AND ABDOMEN

TWO BLACK BANDS ON ABDOMEN

BLACK ANTENNAE

BLACK LEGS

(NO WINGS ON FEMALE; MALE IS WINGED.)

According to legend, the female Red Velvet Ant's sting is strong enough to kill a cow. Actually, it's not, although the sting is extremely painful. But that legend has earned this insect another common nickname: the Cow Killer Ant.

Common Eastern Bumble Bee

Bombus impatiens **ORDER Hymenoptera**
LENGTH 0.33–0.83 in (8.5–21 mm) **HABITAT Meadows,
gardens, and wooded areas with flowering plants** **RANGE Eastern
United States and southeastern Canada** Complete metamorphosis

HAIRY BODY

DARK WINGS

BARBED STINGER AT END OF ABDOMEN

YELLOW THORAX

It does have a painful sting. But the Common Eastern Bumble Bee is also one of the most beneficial insects in the eastern United States. From March to November, it flies around pollinating flowering plants in farms, meadows, suburbs, and urban areas. It thrives wherever it's warm enough and flowers are blooming.

→ LOOK FOR THIS

BUMBLE BEES feed on the pollen and nectar from flowers. To get pollen, they buzz really close to the flowers. The sound vibrations loosen the pollen from the flower's anthers. This process is called "buzz pollination."

Honey Bee

REDDISH BROWN BODIES WITH BLACK BANDS AND YELLOWISH ORANGE RINGS ON THE ABDOMEN

Apis mellifera **ORDER Hymenoptera** **LENGTH 0.39–0.79 in (10–20 mm)**
HABITAT Meadows, gardens, and wooded areas with flowering plants
RANGE Worldwide, except Antarctica Complete metamorphosis

The first Honey Bees appeared in North America in the 17th century. Early settlers brought them over from Europe. Honey Bees live in large colonies inside homes called hives. Life in a hive is very organized. Queen bees lay eggs. Male drones help her reproduce. Workers, or infertile females, maintain the hive and care for growing larvae. These workers have glands on their abdomens that produce wax. They use that wax to build a sheet of six-sided cells called a comb. Larvae grow inside these cells. This is also where the bees store their honey.

HAIRY THORAX

BLACK LEGS WITH POLLEN BASKET ON BACK LEGS

Sweat Bee

Agapostemon splendens **ORDER Hymenoptera**
• **LENGTH 0.39–0.43 in (10–11 mm)** • **HABITAT Clay soil,
sandy banks, and cavities in weeds and shrubs** • **RANGE
North Dakota to Maine, south to Texas and Florida**
• **Complete metamorphosis**

 Sweat Bees are medium-size bees with a natural attraction to human perspiration. They land on your body and lick it to get the salt. Fortunately, they only sting when they're disturbed, and that sting isn't very painful. Most Sweat Bees have brown or black bodies. The species *Agapostemon splendens* is different. Its body is a bright metallic green. How much green the body contains is an easy way to separate the males from the females. Females have a green head, thorax, and abdomen. Males have black and yellow stripes on their abdomen. Sweat Bees build nests in the ground. They are one of the most important pollinators of prairie wildflowers.

INSECT inspector!

Some types of Sweat Bees sneak into the nests of other species and eat the eggs. Then they lay their own eggs, which survive thanks to the food the host left for its own young.

DARK WINGS

HEAD AND THORAX ARE METALLIC GREEN.

YELLOW LEGS WITH BLACK SPOTS

ABDOMEN IS BLACK AND YELLOW STRIPED.

 Laugh Out Loud!

How is a flower like the letter A?

It's always followed by a bee.

Western Carpenter Ant

HAIRY BLACK BODY

Camponotus vicinus ORDER **Hymenoptera** • LENGTH **0.28–0.63 in (7–16 mm)** • HABITAT **Hot, dry areas with sandy to rocky soils** • RANGE **Southwestern Canada, throughout the western United States, to northwestern Mexico** • Complete metamorphosis

The Western Carpenter Ant has a black body with a red thorax. Although these ants don't sting, they do have a strong bite. And when they bite, they inject an acid that makes the wound feel like it's burning. Western Carpenter Ants build nests inside houses and other wooden structures. But the main nest is usually located outside in a dead tree or a woodpile. They build large nesting chambers connected by a series of underground tunnels. Each colony may have up to three dozen queens, so a colony can grow to as many as 100,000 workers!

DULL TO BRIGHT RED THORAX

INSECT inspector!

> Western Carpenter Ants don't eat wood like termites do. But they do dig up and push out dead or decaying wood when they build their tunnels. This can cause a lot of damage to a home. These ants can even damage a new home if the home was built in an area with lots of old trees. Chances are, large colonies of ants already existed when the land was cleared to build the home.

BROWN TO BLACKISH BROWN BODIES

Odorous House Ant

Tapinoma sessile ORDER **Hymenoptera** • LENGTH **0.09–0.13 in (2.5–3.5 mm)** • HABITAT **In homes and outdoors in a wide variety of locations** • RANGE **Throughout the United States** • Complete metamorphosis

If you've ever seen a trail of small brown ants trekking across the kitchen counter-top, chances are good they are Odorous House Ants. Odorous House Ants love sweet stuff. Outside, they eat nectar and honeydew. But inside, they'll head for the sugar you dribbled on the table or the cereal you dropped on the floor. Don't squish these ants! They'll produce an odor with their anal glands that reeks of bad coconut.

FLAT PETIOLE (THIN AREA BETWEEN ABDOMEN AND THORAX)

DARK BROWN BODY WITH TWO SPINES ON THORAX

Pavement Ant

Tetramorium caespitum ORDER **Hymenoptera** · LENGTH **0.1–0.16 in (2.5–4 mm)** · HABITAT **Under sidewalks, stones, pavement, and in the cracks of home foundations** · RANGE **Throughout the United States and southern Canada** · Complete metamorphosis

PALE LEGS

STINGER AT END OF ABDOMEN

To see a Pavement Ant, you usually have to look down. They live under sidewalks, stones, and pavement. Unlike many other ant species, Pavement Ants can have more than one queen in the colony. Because of this, their colonies can be huge. There may be more than 10,000 workers! To protect their home from intruders, workers beat other ants with their antennae. They rip them apart with their mandibles. They will fight until death.

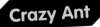

INSECT inspector!

Pavement Ants aren't native to the United States. They come from Europe. It is believed that they crossed the Atlantic Ocean on merchant ships. Merchants coming to America filled their ships with soil to create ballast, or weight. After they arrived, they dumped the soil and filled their ships with goods. The ants were living in the dirt.

EXTREMELY LONG ANTENNAE AND LEGS

Crazy Ant

Paratrechina longicornis ORDER **Hymenoptera** · LENGTH **0.09–0.12 in (2.5–3 mm)** · HABITAT **Agricultural areas and homes** · RANGE **Throughout the United States** · Complete metamorphosis

The easiest way to identify a Crazy Ant is to watch how it moves. These ants don't follow trails like other ants do. They're fast and unpredictable. They scurry about, going wherever they want to. Also unlike other ants, they don't build their nests near where they find food. Instead, workers have to go on long treks. Because of this and their ability to adapt to just about any environment, Crazy Ants can easily become pests. They may invade homes, schools, or hospitals. They can even survive on ships.

DARK BROWN TO BLACKISH BODY WITH WEDGE-SHAPED PETIOLE

Rough Harvester Ant

LARGE BLACK HEAD WITH POWERFUL JAWS

Pogonomyrmex rugosus ORDER **Hymenoptera** • LENGTH **0.2–0.28 in (5–7 mm)** • HABITAT **Desert regions** • RANGE **Southwestern United States** • Complete metamorphosis

On the surface, the home of a Rough Harvester Ant looks like a flattened gravel disk. If you could venture below, you'd see that it is actually a network of underground chambers. Each day, worker ants venture out from that home in search of food. They are scavengers, so they won't turn down a dead insect. But their primary duty is to gather seeds. To harvest these seeds, they bite them off stalks with their strong jaws. Then they carry them back home. Workers husk the seeds in the nest and store them in a mound chamber. They store enough seeds to help the colony survive throughout winter.

BLACK THORAX AND REDDISH BROWN ABDOMEN WITH STINGER

REDDISH BROWN BODIES

Red Imported Fire Ant

Solenopsis invicta ORDER **Hymenoptera** • LENGTH **0.12–0.35 in (3–9 mm)** • HABITAT **Open areas in sunny locations** • RANGE **Southeastern United States, Texas, and California** • Complete metamorphosis

One place you never want to step is in the middle of a Red Imported Fire Ant mound. These ants are small. But they have powerful stingers and they attack in big masses. They came from Brazil in the 1920s or '30s. These predators can easily take down a spider, centipede, or earthworm—even a newly hatched chick. A highly invasive species, they have driven many native ants from their natural territories.

OBVIOUS STINGER ON ABDOMEN

DANGER! NEVER, EVER STEP ON a Red Imported Fire Ant mound. Mature colonies can have up to 240,000 workers. These ants will swarm out of the colony and attack by clamping down on your skin with strong jaws. Then they will inject your body with venom over and over again.

CONSERVING BENEFICIAL INSECTS

Tell your parents to avoid using pesticides and chemicals whenever possible. The same chemicals that kill pests can also kill beneficial species of insects.

MANY BUTTERFLY HABITATS HAVE BEEN DESTROYED. FIND OUT WHAT KIND OF PLANTS YOUR FAVORITE BUTTERFLIES LIKE. THEN PLANT A GARDEN WHERE BOTH LARVAE AND ADULTS CAN FIND FOOD.

As the world's population increases, people use more and more natural resources. Often, this means changing the land around them. While that might seem like the natural thing to do, it's not necessarily what's best for nature. Plants and animals, including insects, need stable homes, too. It's too late to save some species. They've become extinct. But there are many things people can do to protect and preserve the species that are left.

Many insects live in or around water. And everything you drop eventually ends up in a river or stream. Pick up your trash and throw it away. Keep the waterways clean.

Many insects inhabit rotting tree stumps. Rather than burning stumps, encourage adults to let the stumps rot naturally.

Quick ID Guide

Mayflies 16
Giant Mayfly / Ephemeridae

Dragonflies 17-20
Common Green Darner /
Aeshnidae

Damselflies 21-23
Ebony Jewelwing /
Calopterygidae

Stoneflies 26-27
Giant Salmonfly /
Pteronarcyidae

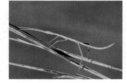

Walkingsticks 28-32
Giant Walkingstick /
Diapheromeridae

Mantids 33-34
Carolina Mantis / Mantidae

Cockroaches 35-37
Oriental Cockroach /
Blattidae

Termites 38-39
Eastern Subterranean
Termite / Rhinotermitidae

Earwigs 42-44
Ring-legged Earwig /
Carcinophoridae

Webspinners 45
Black Webspinner /
Oligotomidae

Grasshoppers 46-49
Velvet-striped Grasshopper
/ Acrididae

Pygmy Mole Crickets 50
Pygmy Mole Cricket /
Tridactylidae

Crickets 51-53
Southern Wood Cricket/
Gryllidae

Katydids 54-55
True Katydid/Tettigoniidae

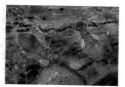
Barklice 58-59
Webbing Barklouse/
Archipsocidae

Booklice 60
Booklouse /Liposcelididae

Lice 61-62
Head Louse/Pediculidae

Thrips 63-64
Western Flower Thrips/
Thripidae

Cicadas 65
17-Year Cicada/Cicadidae

Leafhoppers 66
Grass Sharpshooter/
Cicadellidae

Aphids 67
Pea Aphid/Aphididae

Assassin Bugs 70
Kissing Bug/Reduviidae

Seed Bugs 71
Large Milkweed Bug/
Lygaeidae

Chinch Bugs 72
Hairy Chinch Bug/Blissidae

Bed Bugs 73
Bed Bug / Cimicidae

Stink Bugs 74-75
Harlequin Bug /
Pentatomidae

Plant Bugs 76
Tarnished Plant Bug /
Miridae

Water Striders 77
Water Strider / Gerridae

Water Boatmen 78
Water Boatman / Corixidae

Backswimmers 79
Backswimmer /
Notonectidae

Lacewings 82
Golden-eyed Lacewing /
Chrysopidae

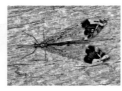

Antlions 83
Antlion / Myrmeleontidae

Mantidflies 84
Green Mantidfly /
Mantispidae

Dobsonflies & Fishflies 85
Eastern Dobsonfly /
Corydalidae

Alderflies 86
Alderfly / Sialidae

Snakeflies 87
Snakefly / Raphidiidae

Beetles 90-103
Sidewalk Carabid/
Carabidae

Hangingflies 106
Black-tipped Hangingfly/
Bittacidae

Scorpionflies 107
Scorpionfly/Panorpidae

Snow Scorpionflies 108
Snow Scorpionfly/Boreidae

Fleas 109
Cat Flea/Pulicidae

Flies 110-117
House Fly/Muscidae

Mosquitoes 118
Northern House
Mosquito/Culicidae

Caddisflies 119
Speckled Peter/
Helicopsychidae

Butterflies 122-126
Common Branded
Skipper/
Hesperiidae

Moths 127-131
Large Tolype Moth/
Lasiocampidae

Sawflies 132
Redheaded Pine
Sawfly/Diprionidae

Wasps 133-138
Eastern
Yellowjacket/
Vespidae

Bees 139-140
Common Eastern
Bumble Bee/Apidae

Ants 141-143
Western Carpenter
Ant/Formicidae

FIND OUT MORE

WANT TO FIND OUT EVEN MORE about insects? Check out these great books, websites, apps, and movies. Be sure to ask an adult to help you search the Web to find the sites listed below.

Books

National Geographic Kids Ultimate Bug-opedia, 2013

Websites

The Bug Club (Amateur Entomologists' Society): www.amentsoc.org/bug-club

The Bug Chicks: thebugchicks.com

BugFacts: www.bugfacts.net

Sci4Kids (United States Department of Agriculture Agricultural Research Service): www.ars.usda.gov/oc/kids/insects/insectintro

Apps

Audubon Insects and Spiders—A Field Guide to North American Insects and Spiders

Atlas: Insects of World

Audubon Butterflies—A Field Guide to North American Butterflies

Insects Pedia

Insects World

Meet the Insects: Village Edition

Mini-Monsters

Movies

DisneyNature: *Wings of Life* (Rated G)

Microcosmos (Rated G)

Glossary

ADAPTATION: A specialized body part or behavior that allows an animal to survive and reproduce in its environment

ARTHROPOD: An invertebrate animal with a segmented body, jointed appendages, and an exoskeleton

BIOLUMINESCENCE: The production of light by a living organism

CAMOUFLAGE: A natural disguise, such as skin color or pattern, that helps an animal blend in with its surroundings

CARCASS: The dead body of an animal

CARRION: The decaying flesh of dead animals

COLONY: A group of the same kind of organism living or growing together

DEFENSE: Body parts, coloring, chemistry, or behaviors that an organism uses to protect itself from attack or harm

ECHOLOCATION: The process of bouncing sound waves off of distant or invisible objects, such as prey, to find them

EGG CASE: A capsule that contains eggs

ENDANGERED: A plant or animal that is at risk of becoming extinct, or no longer existing

ENVIRONMENT: The natural features of a place, such as its weather, landscape, and vegetation

EXOSKELETON: An external supportive covering on an animal's body

EXTINCTION: The state of no longer existing, or being alive. When all the members of a species die out, they are said to go extinct.

FOREWINGS: The two front wings of a four-winged insect

HALTERES: The modified hind wings that help members of the order Diptera balance as they fly

HIBERNATE: To enter an inactive, sleeplike state with lowered body temperature, which aids survival in cold months

HIND WINGS: The two back wings of a four-winged insect

HONEYDEW: A sweet, sticky substance that some insects, such as aphids and some bugs, secrete from their abdomens

HOST: A plant or animal that a parasite feeds on. Typically, the host is somewhat injured or disabled but does not die.

INDICATOR SPECIES: An organism whose presence or absence is used to measure the quality of an environment

INSECT CLASSIFICATION: The grouping of insects based on their relatedness and their physical characteristics

INVASIVE SPECIES: A plant or animal that often is not native to an area or takes over habitat and food resources, harming native species

LARVA: The first stage of an insect's life after it leaves the egg during complete metamorphosis

MANDIBLES: A pair of mouthpart appendages, or jaws, used mainly for tearing and chewing food and carrying objects in insects and some other arthropods

METAMORPHOSIS: A change in structure by an animal that has more than one body form during its life

MIGRATION: The seasonal movement from one location to another

MIMICRY: The similarity in appearance, sound, smell, or behavior of one species to another (or others) that can act to protect one or more species

MOLT: The process in which an insect or other animal sheds or loses a covering of skin, hair, feathers, etc.

NECTAR: A sweet liquid secreted by plants as food to attract animals that will benefit from them

NYMPH: The first stage of an insect's life after it leaves the egg during incomplete metamorphosis

ORDER: One level on which plants and animals are grouped in scientific classification between the levels of class above it and family below it

OVIPOSITOR: The body part that female insects use to lay eggs

PARASITE: An organism that lives on or inside another species of organism (the host) and feeds on it

PHEROMONE: A chemical secreted by an insect or other animal that influences the behavior of other organisms

POLLEN: Tiny grains produced by the male part of flowers that fertilize the future seeds of a plant of the same species

PREDATOR: An animal that hunts other animals for food

PROBOSCIS: The elongated tubular mouthparts that some insects use to drink a liquid meal

PRONOTUM: A hardened plate on the top of the thorax just behind the insect's head that is part of the insect's exoskeleton

PUPA: A life stage of insects with complete metamorphosis during which the larval body is replaced with an adult body. In some insects, the pupa is enclosed in a cocoon.

SCAVENGER: An animal that feeds on dead or decaying matter

SCIENTIFIC NAME: A two-part designation for an animal or plant indicating genus and species

SEGMENTED: Divided into parts

THORAX: The part of the body between the head and the abdomen. In insects, the wings and legs are attached to the thorax.

TYMPANUM: An external hearing structure on insects and some other animals

Index

Boldface indicates illustrations.

Credits

Since 1888, the National Geographic Society has funded more than 12,000 research, exploration, and preservation projects around the world. The Society receives funds from National Geographic Partners, LLC, funded in part by your purchase. A portion of the proceeds from this book supports this vital work. To learn more, visit www.natgeo.com/info.

NATIONAL GEOGRAPHIC and Yellow Border Design are trademarks of the National Geographic Society, used under license.

For more information, visit nationalgeographic.com, call 1-800-647-5463, or write to the following address:

National Geographic Partners
1145 17th Street N.W.
Washington, D.C. 20036-4688 U.S.A.

Visit us online at nationalgeographic.com/books

For librarians and teachers: ngchildrensbooks.org

More for kids from National Geographic: kids.nationalgeographic.com

For information about special discounts for bulk purchases, please contact National Geographic Books Special Sales: specialsales@natgeo.com

For rights or permissions inquiries, please contact National Geographic Books Subsidiary Rights: bookrights@natgeo.com

Editorial, Design, and Production by Potomac Global Media, LLC

National Geographic Partners, LLC, and Potomac Global Media, LLC, would like to thank the following members of the project team: Kevin Mulroy, Barbara Brownell Grogan, William Lamp, Matt Propert, Jane Sunderland, and Tim Griffin.

Art Directed by Kathryn Robbins

Designed by Chris Mazzatenta

Trade Paperback
ISBN: 978-1-4263-2740-7

Reinforced library binding
ISBN: 978-1-4263-2741-4

Printed in China

17/RRDS/1